FOLK, FISH AND FUN

By the same author —
An Airman Marches
Wings Over Westminster

To Janet, with every good wish and much gratitude from. H. B of I. June 1978

FOLK, FISH AND FUN

by

HAROLD BALFOUR
(Lord Balfour of Inchrye, P.C., M.C.)

Foreword by Chapman Pincher

TERENCE DALTON LIMITED
LAVENHAM . SUFFOLK
1978

Published by

TERENCE DALTON LIMITED
LAVENHAM   SUFFOLK

ISBN 0 900963 85 9

Text photoset in 11/12pt Baskerville

Printed in Great Britain at
THE LAVENHAM PRESS LIMITED
LAVENHAM   .   SUFFOLK

The author changing flies

Royalties from this book are being
donated by the author to the
Royal Air Force Benevolent Fund

Contents

Index of Illustrations

Foreword

ANY discerning angler who reads this book of reminiscences by Harold Balfour, as Lord Balfour of Inchrye prefers to be called, will quickly appreciate that he is a fortunate fisherman — fortunate in having fished in so many different and exciting rivers, and thereby having so many memories, but even more fortunate in his belief that just being on any river with a rod in his hand is magic. This, of course, is the essence of angling — being at the side of running water or preferably to my taste, in it. After fifty years of fishing I still experience a thrill of pleasure when wading into a stream to make the first cast of the day.

There is particular magic in a salmon river, as the author expresses so clearly. Apart from the wild scenery usually associated with the salmon, the very names given to the pools where they lurk have charm — like The Otter, Two Stones and the Big Haddie on the Delfur beat of the Spey, which he mentions. As for the Inchmalo beat on the Dee, which he describes so lovingly, I was occasionally that very angler he recalls fishing the opposite side up to my elbows in the water trying to run my bait through a lie while he was fishing "armchair-style" from the other bank with far greater success. The fish lie by the rocks on the Inchmalo side, particularly in the great pool known as the New Fawn as I proved to myself during the only week I had the pleasure of fishing it. On that occasion the new owner of the opposite bank, called Blackhall, where I had previously fished for years, had a party of four rods and they took two salmon in the week. On the Inchmalo side — and the Dee is not wide there — three of us had forty.

Actually the end of Inchmalo's former owner, Jack Howlett, was even more fitting for such an old sportsman than the author states. He had caught a salmon in the Test in the morning and after lunch went out and shot a hare. Then he sat down and died.

I have to agree with the author about the big Norwegian salmon. They tend not to be good fighters but it is immensely sad that most of Norway's rivers are now so overnetted that the runs of fish are small. It is still a great thrill to go, as I did, and get a 30 lb salmon in a week after failing to do so in thirty years elsewhere but to go all that way to catch two or three fish in a week however big is hardly worthwhile.

Iceland, which the author also describes, is altogether more exciting. There most of the rivers are as God made them. The salmon come up unimpeded and in great numbers, as they must have run up the Scottish rivers in the last century. Further there is no pollution and no netting — at least not in the river I fished where my wife and I caught ninety-four salmon in ten days, all on small flies.

It is fitting to end this brief foreword with the memory of my first moment on that Icelandic river, which has an un-pronounceable name but where some of the pools have been named by Englishmen. Starting at Broken Bank I had five salmon in the first five casts. Surely I thought, this must be the greatest taking pool in the world — for it is odd how some promising looking pools hold salmon which do not take readily. I was soon to change my mind. I fished that pool on seven further occasions under apparently similar conditions and never had a touch, though the fish were there. It is this glorious uncertainty of fishing that gives it its abiding charm, as the author of this delightful book so obviously appreciates.

Chapman Pincher.

CHAPTER ONE

My Biggest Ever

L IFE in the political world develops the regrettable habit of the use of trite "bromides" such as "strategy starts where tactics end. Diplomacy starts where strategy ends". Some forty-eight years' service in both Houses of Parliament and I have heard, and I fear, used myself, far too many of these rather pert sayings. I could give a whole list of them but I only want to quote one more to which I really do take exception and reject absolutely. "All fisherman are liars. Some lie more than others". On behalf of my brother anglers I stoutly deny the charge. If sometimes there is some small exaggeration at the size or weight, surely this is permissible outside the question, "When does exaggeration stop and lying commence?" Anyhow in this book I do promise that I have tried to keep strictly within the bounds of truth as far as memory of fifty years and more of fishing in several lands allows.

The happiness of fishing does not depend on size of catch or comparison with what others have done. To me competitive amateur sport, be it in shooting, fishing, ski-ing or anything else, is repellent. At once pleasure yields place to envy of someone else's luck. Of course, on a salmon river when the other fellow has landed three fish and you have not had a touch, one wishes for a share in his good fortune. But that is not jealousy so long as the other fellow's success brings you joy. I hope that I have gone well down the road of contentment when I say that I get a greater kick out of helping, advising, watching some young person hooking and playing their first salmon than catching a fish myself. I know I share with the vast majority of fishermen that riverside thought-to-oneself: "I will gladly give up any chance today of a fish if the powers-that-be will give young David my chance." The wonderful feeling of peace beside running water can be desecrated by resentment at the achievement of others. For me just to be by

1

running water is the foundation of happiness of the day. In my mind, as I write these words, I have a picture of the green fields, hills and woods of the Tweed as it courses through Mertoun towards the sea. There are dark mysterious pools: there are rapid runs beyond the shingly bank, then the fast tumble round and over rocks and always the glorious autumn colourings. There is the Shin with its almost threatening rock cliffs with the climb over what we term the "hump" when we pick our way carefully upwards, each foot finding safe anchorage in the rocky steps before we try the next one. The rod is in the left hand and with the right we are hanging on to the guide wire. At the top we can look down through the deep clear smooth water to see the big rocks of the river bed and one, two, or three great big fish relaxing lazily on the bottom. Below we come to the lovely Angus Pool which is welcoming, gentle, and nearly always fruitful. I know the little Borgie winding through the heather. Sutherland has so many lovely rivers each with its own character which you quickly learn to appreciate as well as learning the pools and the favourite lies of the fish. It is, as one gets older, that each day on the river becomes more precious. Once beside the river worries of the overdraft, the children's problems, business difficulties, the political situation; these and other such thoughts just fade away. One becomes just the happy fisherman.

Having written some warning words about memory and exaggeration with passage of time, let me start with an account of the biggest fish I have ever caught or am likely to catch. And here there is nothing but the truth as the photograph in this book proves.

In the winter of 1944 I found myself on the Gold Coast — now Ghana. The long history of how I found myself there does not belong to this tale of the big fish. Enough to say that I served in the Royal Flying Corps and the Royal Air Force through the First World War, and in a book published by Hutchinson's in 1973 *Wings over Westminster* I told of those early flying days and how, as M.P. for the Isle of Thanet, I became Under-Secretary of State for Air in Mr Chamberlain's Government and stayed there in Mr Churchill's administration until the autumn of 1944. By then the war was surely, if slowly, drawing to a close in Europe. The Prime Minister told me that he contemplated no Government reconstruction before the defeat of Germany and for someone who had been too long at the Air

2

My Biggest Ever

The author's wife, Maina, at the old camp, Gander

The author fishing the Shin   *Photograph by J. T. Learwood*

The author, Vancouver Island, 1922

"Out She Comes" — the author gaffing a salmon

The author, David with his first salmon, George Murray

The author's wife fishes the Bend Pool, Dee

The Ardmiddle beat on the Deveron

K. C. Irving (second from left) and party: the author on extreme left

Fishing the Testwood, Hampshire.   *By courtesy of The Field*

Ministry the only office of Cabinet rank which he would be likely to have vacant was to succeed Lord Swinton as Resident Minister, West Africa. Sixteen years in the House of Commons, six and a half years in Office and a constituency ravaged by enemy air raids, depopulated for security reasons and needing youth and energy for political leadership in post war reconstruction. This was my position. I could take the appointment, but how could I go to my voters and say, "Goodbye boys. I am off to West Africa. I will be back on polling day and you will vote for me, won't you?" I felt I should have got the dusty answer that I deserved. I felt also that I could no longer face the 5.08 p.m. train from Cannon Street to Margate every Friday evening; attend the Mayor's banquet or some other dinner function; have to make a speech; go on to drink beer and more beer at the British Legion or the Conservative Clubs; followed by Saturday morning around employment exchanges, interviewing constituents, lunch with some kind folk; in the afternoon watch a football match in which I was not really interested and then maybe around 7.00 p.m. become my own master. The prospect was just too grim, so for me it was goodbye to the House of Commons and to my brave constituents who had endured physical dangers and economic ruin. The Prime Minister wrote me a letter to say that at the dissolution he would recommend me to His Majesty for a peerage and so I would go to the House of Lords. All of which happened in due course.

Meanwhile, from November 1944 to the end of the war I had my West African stint. The Resident Minister's parish ran from Dakar through Gambia, Sierra Leone, the Gold Coast and Nigeria, with a sphere of administrative responsibility to include the Belgian Congo. To cover this terrific area I had the privilege and enjoyment of a beautifully equipped DC3 and a first class crew, and so managed to get around in some degree of comfort and, for those days, at a good speed of around 160 miles per hour.

Before I flew out in the Dakota via Gibraltar and Oran to Accra I had made some enquiries as to what sort of sea fishing there might be on the Gold Coast. I had little encouragement from those I asked. No one seemed to know anything, until I came across an official in the Colonial Office who told me about a Gold Coast Governor of many years past. Somewhere down the line was a story that this Governor said there was fantastic

3

tarpon fishing at the mouth of the Volta River. Beyond this passed-on rumour I could learn nothing and it was not until I followed this up from local Gold Coast sources that I found out some more. Governor Hodgson (I think that was his name) was apparently a very eccentric gentleman. He lived as a bachelor, whether single or with a wife in the background I do not know, for he spurned living in the official Government House, preferring rooms over the stable with two black ladies for his comfort. His only form of transport was walking on his two legs. When he left the Coast he also left a reputation of having walked over pretty well every part of the Gold Coast. He was a rough and tough man but loved by all tribal Africans, both in the northern and southern territories. It was he who reported the tarpon and claimed to have caught several in the river estuary.

Today I expect the sparsely populated little African village of Ada is at the centre of the great Volta River Hydro-Electric Scheme and that the mouth of the Volta River would be unrecognisable as I knew it. In 1944 it was a swift running natural outflow with the Ada village on the right bank and palm tree scrub country opposite on the left bank. The estuary itself was perhaps a third of a mile across. Looking towards the sea over the Ada quay one could see the white waves breaking over the sand bar some half mile below the village. Here the river finally ended and met the breakers of the South Atlantic. With the tide on the ebb one could see down onto the sandy bottom through clear water about eight feet deep and running like a fast Scottish river.

Before leaving London I had gone to Farlow's, then in Panton Street, and invested in a very secondhand deep sea fishing rod, leather shoulder harness with butt socket, a huge reel and a line of what strength I do not know. I bought some big hooks, yards of piano wire and oversize swivels to make up into traces.

Resident Ministers' headquarters were at Achimota College about three miles out of Accra. I lived in a pleasant bungalow overlooking the golf course which had previously been the Headmaster's house.

All this fishing gear I had put away in a corner and forgot about it for the first several weeks until someone brought to mind Governor Hodgson. There and then I decided to explore this Ada story. The next Saturday I set off for Ada with two

4

companions in two motor cars, with lots of sandwiches and beer.

It was a dull, flat, hot drive of about seventy miles down the coast. The District Officer had been warned of our expedition and had arranged for two long canoes complete with paddling crews to be ready for us. Each canoe was manned by six Africans, naked except for brief loin cloths, but with one superior who sported patched-up old dungarees and a shirt. He, I was told, was "boss boy" and a local employee of the United Africa Company. He, alone, understood a little bit of English and could speak a few broken words. He took his place in the bow as Admiral of the Fleet and coxswain of the canoe from which I was to fish. Before leaving Accra we had visited the fish market and brought with us a bucketful of small fish, about herring size, to use as bait. Rods were put up. Hooks were baited with the dead fish. Leads were fixed on the wire traces and off we pushed.

We decided that both canoes should troll back and forth across the estuary where the tide was running out strongly. Within minutes of getting my line out I felt a good pull. I struck but nothing happened. The pull was not strong enough for a really big fish so I guessed it would have been a barracuta. The bait was lightly marked and that was all. During the next hour or so trolling backwards and forwards across the estuary mouth each of us had several strikes but nothing took hold. I had seen no fish showing but just as I was beginning to think that big fish legend was an old wives tale, a huge great head and back showed about fifty yards up river from our canoes. It looked like something between a giant salmon rise and a porpoise showing. Then another and another. My heart stood still for here were the legendary tarpon; a shoal of them. We headed the canoes to where they had shown. I felt a strong steady pull on my line. Something much bigger than a barracuta. I struck but again nothing. I had maybe three or four of these great strikes. Alas; that day I had to get back to Accra by a fixed time so we could do nothing except pack it in and motor the long run back, defeated but also determined to come back to the attack. We were all sadly puzzled at our complete failure to get hold of one of these monsters. Anyhow, we now knew where the tarpon could be found at the right tide.

It was a good month before I could get back to Ada and this

time I was alone. Meanwhile, I had been thinking out where our tactics had been wrong and how to put matters right. I decided to try treating the tarpon like fishing for salmon with greased line and small fly. Here you have to let the fish rise, take the fly and do nothing except let the fish pull out the loop of slack line your left hand is holding. Then, when you feel the fish, you tighten on him. Always when fishing with floating or greased line for salmon once I have got a fish on I give a good yank just to make sure the fly has really gone home in the fish's mouth. The tarpon, I decided, were to be treated in the same way.

At Ada I found waiting for me the same crew and the same "boss boy". We started off across the estuary and I paid out line for the troll, but when I had let out enough, some twenty to thirty yards, I coiled another ten to fifteen feet of line by my feet on the bottom of the canoe. I held this lightly in my left hand to prevent any more running out from the pull of the canoe. We had been trolling for about twenty minutes when I felt a strong pull on the line. I let it run through my fingers and at the same time the excited "boss boy" shouted, "Feesh, feesh!" and the rest of the crew set up an almighty chatter. I sat absolutely still while the line ran out quite slowly and gently. Just as the last of the fifteen feet or so was unwinding off the bottom of the canoe I took both hands to the rod, put the reel brake at half strength, and gave one tremendous strike. The next second several things seemed to happen all at once. The rod was almost jerked out of my arms, the reel screamed, the line tore off the drum and a great bar of silver hurled itself out of the water, not behind the canoe where my line was still cutting the water, but way far out on the flank. The fish must have done a high speed circle under the water directly it got the bait in its mouth. The fish gave me a second's grace; just long enough to let me do two most urgent tasks. First, with fumbling trembling hands I got the rod butt into the shoulder harness socket and, secondly, I slammed the reel brake hard on. Then the true fight started with a series of rushes, usually finishing with a great leap into the air. Luckily the hook held and whenever the fish eased even for a moment I managed to shorten the line by a yard or so. Gradually this shortening process gave me three or four yards recovery each time the fish rested. He was starting to tire. After about thirty minutes of piscatorial fireworks I began to feel I had him under some degree of control. I knew by now from what we had seen that I was into a really big tarpon. Soon I began thinking ahead about how and where we could ever land him. There was no question of trying to get this monster into the canoe. With his weight and size he would have had the canoe and all of us straight into the water. To bring him alongside within gaffing distance would also be dangerous; one flick with his tail or one roll would swamp the canoe and shoot all of us into the fast running tidal stream with very little hope of ever making the shore. "Boss boy" had brought along a six or seven foot pole on the end of which he had lashed a bill-hook and this had to be our gaff. I decided the only hope was to land him from the sandy beach on the left bank.

Slowly we worked the canoe towards the shore with the fish following quite docilely, now on a fairly short line. He was either tired and resting or playing cunning. For my part, while he was in this gentle mood, I was careful not to tease him unnecessarily. Even in this estuary there were quite considerable waves lapping the sandy shore, but the canoe boys with great skill under the "Admiral's" shouted orders, rode the canoe on top of a wave into knee deep water. Holding the rod upright I jumped ashore but this was just too much for the tarpon. He had got his second wind and off he went, making for the sand bar and the wide open sea beyond. Puffing and blowing I ran as fast as I could along the beach, still with the rod upright and the fish pulling out more and more line. If he had gone on, I could have done nothing except cut the line when he got near the bar. Anyhow, before he reached the danger area he thought better of it, turned about and started up stream. I played him hard on an ever shortening line and called "boss boy" to my side. By now the canoe had been pulled up out of the water and the crew were all jumping round me and shouting with excitement. I told "boss boy" that when I had the fish really beat with no life left in him I would reel in hard, bringing him into the shallow water on top of one of the waves. I managed to do this by good luck. At the right moment I pulled the fish onto the crest of the biggest wave I had been watching for over several minutes. When the wave broke, the fish was lying in the shallow water, floating motionless a few feet in front of me. "Boss boy" rushed into the water and with his bill-hook truly gaffed the fish in the wretched victim's eye. No matter, the fish was safely pulled in. I firmly believe that gallant fish was dead already when I brought him in on the crest of the wave. He had killed himself fighting, for once we had him lying on the sand he never stirred.

We managed to get the fish aboard the canoe. When we reached the quay we weighed him on the United Africa Company's commercial scales. He just topped 185 lbs. I got the boys to strap him on the roof of my car for the journey back to Accra where he was duly photographed by a battery of cameras from every position and finally given to our African household staff as a present. Quite a few Africans that evening must have had a good meal.

Only once more did I have the chance of using the heavy rod and tackle again — in Africa or indeed anywhere else.

One day in 1939 in the smoking room of the House of Commons I was talking fishing with a very dear and respected friend, the late Captain Charles Waterhouse, M.P. He told me how he had been in Khartoum just before the war and had gone south of the city for some miles to the newly built Nile barrage, the Sennar Dam. He had fished for big Nile perch off one of the sluices. I forget now what he told me he had caught, but it had all been great fun with a big spoon bait worked in the heavy water below the sluice gates. I had stored this story in my memory and now in 1944 I was stopping off for the night on my way up to the Middle East Headquarters. The Governor of Sudan and Her Excellency were my kind hosts at the "Palace". I asked about this dam and was told that it was within easy car distance so in the evening I went back to the airport, unloaded my rod and tackle off our Dakota and brought it to the Palace. At dawn the next day I was driven to the barrage. Some of the sluice gates were open and a foaming torrent of water poured out from each of these gates. At right angles to the barrage a number of stone piers ran out for about thirty or forty yards and between any two piers the water ceased to boil and foam so that by the time the piers ended the streams were coming down in the form of unbroken rivers without frothing and boiling. It was from the end of one of these piers that I thought I could work my spoon across and down the flow. It was in fact just harling from a fixed position. There was plenty of current for the spoon to do its wobble perfectly. I started with a short line then let it out yard by yard, myself standing on the bottom edge of the pier and bringing the spoon across and through the current. About the third time I was doing this, something took it with a bang. Let me confess the fish gave no great thrill. It never showed or jumped. It did a few rushes downstream then it just lay deep in the water like a great dead weight. After about twenty minutes I handed the gaff I carried to the Loch attendant who had been detailed to look after me and he neatly gaffed a 65 lb Nile perch. That was all. Rather dull and disappointing. I put the fish in the back of the car and at the Palace I handed it over to Her Excellency who was delighted to have it as a raffle prize at her Red Cross Sale later in the same day.

So ended the very secondhand rod and tackle from C. Farlow & Sons. What happened to the lot in later years, I just don't remember.

CHAPTER TWO

In the Beginning

In the beginning it was a bent pin.

SUTTON, Surrey is today a built-over residential suburb of South London. Street after street of neat houses! Its own shopping area! Wide roads and highway intersections. It is hard now to imagine Sutton as a country village. Green farmland fields and, above all, a beautiful little river with crystal clear pure water well stocked with brown trout running up to 2 lb weight. Yet that was Sutton; in the year 1903. A soldier uncle at the War Office had rented a charming country house through the gardens of which flowed the perfect little stream. Two small nephews, five and seven, came to stay: my elder brother and myself. He, as eldest and wisest, had a cheap little reel and line. Junior had to be content with a long garden stick with a piece of string tied on the end. Senior had a hook. Junior a bent pin, but both had a worm on hook and pin. Uncle was away at his duties. Nephews had heard him talk of the big trout in the pool at the bottom of the garden where, shaded by trees, the monster he was determined to lure to his fly lay lazily all day in the deep of the pool. Uncle had declared his firm intention of catching him when he rose to his late evening meal of fly. Nephews sneaked down and crept to the bank, hidden by the bush. There he was on the gravel bed. Junior was granted by a kindly elder the privilege of being the first to tempt with the luscious worm. The long stick was poked out through the branches of the protective bush. Gently the worm was lowered into the water a couple of feet above the fish. At once there was a rush by the fish. He took the worm in one gulp. Junior was too surprised, excited, scared, to do anything except give one strong upward heave. Somehow the string held and the wretched fish did a parabola in the air, landing on the bank well clear of the water: Both boys hurled themselves on the flapping monster and smothered it with their hands. Proudly the two returned to the house carrying the prize. No great congratulations from Auntie when she had listened to the saga of its capture. Only, "Your Uncle won't be at all pleased. That was the one he has been trying for every night last week. You had better explain to him when he comes back tonight from the War Office." That evening two little boys formed up to confess to Uncle, displaying before his astonished eyes a fat brownie of 2½ lbs presented on a platter. When Uncle learnt where and how the fish had been caught there was a deathly silence. Was it to be an explosion of anger or of laughter? Uncle being a true sportsman opted for the latter. All was forgiven. The result was a promise of proper fishing tuition and a present next day of two lovely little trout rods with proper reels, lines, gut casts and some flies. "Now boys," said Uncle, "stop poaching and we will teach you on the lawn first to cast properly and then I will take you to the river."

This first adventure at the age of five set me on the road of joyful fishing from which I have never strayed over so many years.

My next memory is of the burn which ran through the property of Torrance, East Kilbride in Lanarkshire which belonged to a fierce bearded Colonel Harington Stuart, Uncle Eddie, a man much older than my aunt who he had married. My brother and I were sent up to Torrance for school holidays. I was seven and already at a preparatory boarding school. The burn ran through a cutting, then over a waterfall. Below this there was a deep round pool which held the largest trout in the burn; maybe 6 to 8 ozs. My brother and I held this pool in some terror. The sky could scarcely be seen for trees, the depth could to us have been bottomless; the water was inky black. It could scare little boys. We christened it "the dark and dreary pool" and pretended that it was the centre of an impregnable fortress and determined that no one should pass the barriers we built of logs along the path running about 30 feet above the pool. Down the path strode a heavily moustached figure. It was Uncle Eddie's guest, Lord Dundonald, who we boys only knew as a great Boer War General, now in retirement and devoting his energies and resources to the commercial development of the Dundonald combined kettle and teapot. When the water was boiling you tipped the kettle spout down and the boiling water ran into a teapot held in place on a sort of tripod. The kettle movement released from a canister fixed above the teapot a measure of tea. When the water level in the teapot reached a particular point the teapot lid fell into place.

11

The teapot with tea made was then lifted off its tripod ready for pouring. I gathered later that this invention of the distinguished General was not a commercial success. Anyhow with his great strategic knowledge General The Earl of Dundonald squashed in six sentences the confidence in the design of a defensive fort of two little boys of seven and nine. From every quarter we were vulnerable to our attacking enemies. We felt a bit sad but also rather proud that a great General had given us his appreciation of the situation. We went on with casting our flies or worm into "the dark and dreary pool", even if vulnerable to invaders. I guess we pretty near cleaned out that pool of trout by the end of the holidays.

School holidays up to when I was seventeen in 1914 gave me not many chances of fishing. We had a house at Westward Ho! in the pre-1914 war years. The reservoir up behind Bideford had brown trout at 2/6d a day. Some North Devon and Exmoor streams gave us small trout but, looking back, those were pretty dull fishing years for a growing lad.

The early twenties really started me off on my serious fishing career. In those days there was a dry fly stream at West Drayton, just by Hayes. It was run by an Austrian who was reported to feed his stock trout with horse flesh. This may well have been so for they ran to 3 and 4 lbs. The best time on the river was when the mayfly hatched in early June. This has well been labelled "Duffers' fortnight". At West Drayton every fish was a "taker" and the hatch tremendous. I think we only paid about £1 a day for really rewarding water. The water keeper told me how in the living room of his cottage he finished his tea, lit his pipe and ticked off the day when he had seen the first mayfly. Their sad little one day of life is usually mid-May to late June, depending on weather. Alas, today that stream is polluted; the pretty country fields through which it meandered are no longer but now housing and industrial factories. From my West Drayton days and from later experiences on other rivers I know how telegrams used to flash north, east, south and west to lawyers, doctors, politicians, business men and hundreds of others. Just two words: "Mayfly up". Today in the south of England it is hard to find a decent hatch on waters where in years past, thousands would float gently downstream, victims of big fish that for most of the year live in dark deep pools, never showing, spurning fly artificial and natural, many of them turning cannibal feeders except in this mayfly time.

My fishing education proceeded but by 1924 still not a salmon to my name. However, I had passed through one experience that always shall I remember. My cousin, Melville Balfour, had taken a lodge somewhere up in the hills above Kingussie. The terrain was high for we climbed up after ptarmigan. By the high up lodge was a loch of about 20 acres. Someone in London, when he heard of where I was going said to me, "Never mind about trout up there. Try that loch for really big pike." So off I went in the row boat to troll a minnow. Within ten minutes there was a tremendous strike. I seized the little spinning rod which was bent nearly double. At the end of the first run a huge pike jumped just like a salmon. After about ten minutes hard fight I had the fish beat by the boat. I had no gaff and my trout net was far too small so I worked the boat to the shore and finally beached a 12 lb pike. Fat, beautiful shape, perfect condition. In this clear cold water high up in the hills I found that these pike played like salmon and quite unlike any pike from southern ponds or rivers. Over the next few days I had tremendous sport with these clean fish. We found, too, that they baked and ate beautifully. I had never met pike like these before or since. I only wish I could help any reader by remembering the name of that lodge, but, alas, it has gone from me.

My next adventure was an all-night run starting late on a Friday to Blagdon. In 1926 or so Blagdon was a very different proposition to the much fished, much stocked Blagdon of today. Three of us put up at the little Mendip Bungalow Hotel high above the lake. That famous character, Donald Carr, alas dead for many years now, was in charge. About six other men were fishing. There were just two boats. By dawn we were at the lakeside by the Rickford Pipe down which the hill waters rushed to the lake. At first light every morning we found fish moving in the flow below the pipe exit. Usually we managed to hook and sometimes land a big brownie. My best was a 7½ lb fish of which proudly I had a cast made on a wood mount. For years, whatever house I was living in this cast had a place of honour.

Later came the first invitation to the Spey at Fochabers which I have described in "The Chapter of Shame". From this time on I reckoned my apprenticeship was over. I was properly launched on my serious fishing career.

CHAPTER THREE

Oh What A Beautiful Morning

Oh what a beautiful day—
I've got a wonderful feeling
Everything's going my way

AND it certainly did. I had to be in London for that August Bank Holiday Saturday and Sunday. All day happy holiday folk in their cars big, little, open, closed, stately chauffeur driven Rolls and Bentleys, little family cars packed with children, bed rolls and beach buckets, streamed down Kensington High Street out to somewhere in the country. I was stuck here due to business but still I had joy in my heart. I knew my turn was coming on Bank Holiday Monday. I had been asked by my good friend and colleague on the Board of British European Airways, Sir Walter Edmonson, to come over to Northern Ireland for a day on the Bann. This was before the present "troubles" when Ulster welcomed visitors not with bombs and bullets but with a smile and, if you carried a rod, with a wishful "Good fishing your Honour". Never having cast a line in Ulster this was, for me, a great day of exploration and adventure.

I set the alarm clock for 5 a.m. but anticipation was such that at 4 a.m. I was wide awake. The next hour was a sort of stop-go of dozing. By 5.30 a.m. I was downstairs standing on the doorstep ready for the car that was to pick me up. Like all good fishermen, the night before I had got ready and checked all my tackle. Years ago I learnt by bitter lesson the extreme importance of this. I had been invited for a day on the Bossington water on the Test. I knew the stretch fairly well so after meeting the keeper he left me to go to the river and went about his other duties. When I got to the river bank I saw some good fish rising. Hurriedly I put up my rod and went to my fishing bag to get out the reel and line. Nothing. Just nothing there. I emptied fly boxes and all the odd bits and pieces every fisherman seems to collect like oil, amadou, scissors, nylon.

But still nothing. The blow struck hard. I knew now for certain I had left the reel and line at home. Two hours in the car and a walk of three-quarters of a mile from the keeper's house to my beat and here I was at 11 a.m. useless to myself and everyone else. Slowly and sadly I trudged back. Mrs Keeper said her husband had gone off in the car to Winchester. No; she didn't know when he would be back. No; she didn't know where any of his tackle was kept. His gear was all locked up. No; she didn't know where I could borrow a reel. Maybe I could have thrown myself on the mercy of the landlord of the Grosvenor Hotel, Stockbridge Headquarters of the Houghton Club — or maybe found a tackle shop which would help me out. By the time I had got back to the place where I had left my gear on the river bank it was lunch time. Mournfully I ate my sandwiches and by then the rise had stopped. The river could have been dead of fish for all the movement and there would be nothing doing until the evening. I had to be back in London not too late so sadly I packed my gear, walked back to my car, pointed the nose to London and started for home. Lesson learnt — well learnt.

So on this day to the Bann I knew if I failed to move a fish it would not be for the lack of rod, reel, line or flies, or spinning gear for I took with me a 9′ 6″ spliced-joint greenheart Grant Vibration fly rod and a light spinning rod with the Fleuger reel I always used and had learnt pretty good accuracy by thumb breaking the drum at the right moment to prevent an over-run. Except for the milk vans and a few cars or bicycles clear roads with a beautiful sky. I was, of course, early for the 6.30 a.m. take-off. But fortified with tea and toast I got on board the great lumbering Vanguard. One hour five minutes later we touched down at Belfast's Nutts Corner Airport and never did eggs and bacon taste better than in the airport restaurant. It was still not yet 7.45 a.m. My very dear host had sent his car for the 45 minutes' run to Cullybackey where we were to pick him up. Through peaceful Antrim and Ballymena, names of places read now with almost daily horror and grief at some ghastly pointless outrage. We turned off the main road down to the fishing hut as we left the houses of Ballymena which were mostly villa pattern architecture. Simple, neat, each with little garden carefully tended, the big modern factory dominating the centre of the town. I believe they made cigarettes there. As we passed through, friendly old and young waved to Walter and our car. Now when I read of some horrible death-dealing senseless murder in Ballymena my mind goes back to the happy little town that bright early morning.

We were to fish the stretch below the weir through which the water of the river Bann passes out of Loughneagh. Directly after the weir the river narrowed to some 80 yards width. The water level that day was low but even so there was a good stream running below the hut that looked lovely and which the ghillie with Irish optimism told us "was just full of fish". As we put up our rods I had the thrill of seeing several salmon show and a few perfect head and tail rises. We were to share the boat; one in the bows and one in the stern. Walter had not got out the full length of his cast before he was into a fish. Most of them averaged about 8 lbs and a week before he had the tremendous total for one day of 23 salmon between two rods. I could not help wondering as he hooked this first if we were in for the same sort of day. Alas; even as the ghillie was working the boat to the shore the fish jumped and was off. These little fish have tender mouths and Walter was using a fairly hefty rod. However, in a very short time he hooked and landed a well-shaped fish of about 10 lbs. For me only one pluck at my shrimp fly on the floating line. Then a good rise and my first fish of the day was on. We got the boat to the bank and from the shore I played him out until the seven pounder was safely in the net on the bank but, alas, not in the bag. As the ghillie unhooked the fly the fish took violent evasive action and with one leap was out of the net and with a second was right back into the river. The brave ghillie threw himself on the fish but the fish was just too quick and cunning. He shot away down stream with an astonished ghillie saying: "Shure — and this has never happened to me in all me loife befor." But it had now. One more on the fly to Walter and then at 11.30 a.m. they just went dead. Nothing showed and if we had not known the fish were there we might have thought the river empty. Walter then showed me the shrimp technique. Use the fly so long as there is a chance but don't go flogging the water. Better to change the lure. Now we mounted two tiny shrimps and let out line yard by yard into the stream working the rod tip and jerking the line with hand tugs. The fish just nibbled, sometimes for minutes, before one dared to risk a strike. At lunch-time using this method we had six fish in the boat. By the time we had finished our lunch the wind had risen blowing up stream. On the ghillie's advice we outboarded half a mile downstream where the ghillie said: "Begorrah, Sirs, if there's fish here, why down there they'd just jostle each other." But gloomily he added: "For shure though they won't take with this wind." The stream when we got there proved too slack to carry a fly. Fish showed all round us but just took no notice of our shrimp fly worked in the way I have described. I put up a spinning rod and first cast with a No. 3 "Mep" resulted in a good pull. Next cast and I was into a fresh fish of 9 lbs which we landed. Was this, I asked myself, the answer to a fisherman's prayer? Were we about to scoop the pool? Quickly Walter followed by putting on the "Mep". At once he had one. Two more and bang; they shut up as tight as clams. Nothing would tempt them so back we motored for half a mile upstream back to the hut. We decided to have just another brief go with the fly in the stream before packing it in and so we added one more each giving a total bag of eleven for the day. Not too bad we felt as we, and the ghillie too, downed a good dram of Irish whisky.

I was working on a tight time schedule with an hour and a half's run back to Nutts Corner. Grateful goodbyes; another final go at the bottle as our ghillie took down my rods and I arrived at the Airport just before reporting time. This time a full Vanguard and I wondered if any of the other 128 passengers felt as happy and tired as I did. London Airport 8.30 p.m. Home 9.15 p.m. Bath and bed 9.45. Asleep 9.48. Quite a day.

CHAPTER FOUR

Escape to the Coho

THIS is the story of how I got on terms with the Pacific Coho Salmon, now the centre of controversy as to whether or not it should be introduced in our Atlantic Salmon Waters.

It all happened many years ago. The First World War and my twenty-first birthday had finished only three years before. Use of military rank titles was still the fashion. "If you were the only girl in the world" outranked "Yes, we have no bananas" in any popular song poll.

We who had served in France had yet to come to our full senses and adapt to a peace time life, the prospects of which we had discounted for the past four years of war. At Oxford and Cambridge the last of the ex-Service undergraduates were coming down and in their places came a new post-war generation which grew to resent these elderly warriors who on the slightest provocation would launch out into long boring war reminiscences. After three pretty busy years as a fighter pilot on the Western Front the impact of peace left me dazed. My great wish was to go on with the flying I loved but without a Fokker on my tail or the bursting of anti-aircraft shells in my ears. If I could be allowed just to do this I would be happy. Miners' strikes, railway strikes, unemployed marches; these and the social changes around us were not for me to concern myself with. As long as I could go on giving flying instruction to the cadets of the recently opened R.A.F. College at Cranwell in Lincolnshire, I told myself, I would be content. By 1929 I felt that the isolation of Cranwell was not enough. I could not avoid reading and hearing of great events going on outside my closed world. Each week I read of contemporaries throwing up good jobs "to get out of the rat race" as they would now put it.

Two good friends of mine in the war days had done just this and had landed up in Vancouver Island. Why not, they wrote to me, come out and join them in a land development scheme they had in mind. I applied for and was granted unpaid leave.

At Victoria, B.C., Eddie Clark and Hugh Robb met me off the boat from Vancouver. Both had been at Eton together. Both had been fighter pilots. Both had won the M.C.

The joint venture was to buy some fifteen acres of scrub land, clear the trees and bush: to build an access road and then hope to sell the complete property to one of the many families coming west to retire on Vancouver Island after a life in the harsh mid-Canada wheat belt provinces. Our site was at Metchosin, a district some twenty miles west of Victoria and a mile inland from the sea and no other house within a mile. A rough track ran through the bush and it was off this we intended to develop and build our house. We bought a secondhand tractor and some other equipment and started on clearing. We chose the site of the house, but our first job was to make an access road. We laid the foundations for a simple four-room wooden frame house, to have water, gas lighting and all modern conveniences. Both Eddie and Hugh were far better craftsmen than I was so my main chores were as general handy-man and driving the tractor on clearing work. The house grew. The living room had a fine open brick fireplace and of wood logs for burning there were plenty. Water came from two large storage tanks. We had sliding windows in their frames taken from the cabins of a steamer wrecked further up the coast. Outside we had chicken and goat sheds but the crowning triumph was a three piece bathroom. It was a red letter day when we christened the W.C. with a ceremonial first plug pull and cistern flush.

It was not work all the time.

The rocky sea coast beach was only a mile off. I knew the bay was a favourite spot for the Japanese boats fishing commercially for salmon. I got hold of an old rowing boat, put up a fly rod and mounted a leader with Swivel and Stuart Spoon. Off the shore about twenty yards wide ran a belt of floating sea weed known as kelp with roots fixed in the sea bed. I rowed to just beyond the line of kelp, let out twenty yards of line and started on a course parallel to the sea weed. My rod nearly jumped out of the boat. The reel screamed in protest at the speed it was expected to turn. The fish jumped — a bar of bright silver. I played it carefully and after some five minutes of jumps and dashes, netted a lovely Coho of about eight pounds. Now that all on our own we had found this wonderful sport we were at it nearly every evening. Soon we found an even more exciting variation. Instead of trolling a spoon we tied the boat to the kelp at a point where the fish ripped past like the stream of a Scotch river. Discarding the spoon we put on a big No. 1 or No. 2 Alexander or a local buck-tail fly. The Coho took these just as well as the spoon so our fun was multiplied several times over. It would be a bad evening if we did not have three or four fish in the boat by the time we came in. Very quickly we learnt how to change our catches for much needed and welcome dollars and cents. The Jap boats cruised up and down trolling twelve Stuart Spoons from two outboard booms. When a fish took, a bell on the bridge rang and an indicator showed on which spoon the fish had taken. There was no nonsense about playing a fish. Their lines and leaders were coarse and the hooked fish was just hauled straight in, knocked on the head and thrown into the fish locker. Now all we had to do was to row alongside and hand over our catch. It was weighed and we were given a chit to its value which we could cash in at the general store for household supplies. These Coho made fine eating but only when fresh out of the sea. As they enter the mouth of river or stream up which they go to spawn a sad transformation takes place. They lose freshness and colour and their flesh becomes soft and tasteless. Thousands die as they huddle and struggle to get up some small stream. I have walked across these streams, maybe only inches deep with not enough water to cover their backs, having to kick aside the dead and dying and rotting.

A last word on the Coho. The proposal to introduce them over here has raised alarm and a storm of protest from every quarter as being a danger to the Atlantic salmon food supplies and spawning grounds. As a result, the corporation proposing to import Coho as an experiment have agreed to such strict government control and supervision that it seems any such dangers are checked so far as this initial experiment is concerned. On the other hand the Coho does supply much of the tinned salmon market over here. The experiment of Coho introduction in some American East Coast rivers is reported not to have proved to be the expected menace to the Atlantic salmon and looks like being successful. Coho supporters feel no harm to food supplies or spawning beds of Atlantic fish would come, while a new source of food would become available. It is all so technical and too expert for me. All I would say is that in its Pacific waters I know the Coho is a grand sporting fish. But let us certainly take no risks. Our poor salmon today have already too many enemies to contend with.

Nearly a year had passed. War memories had dimmed. War weary men had gone. The three of us agreed that life for each of us held more than in the backwoods of Vancouver Island. We were still young. We were not fools. Each felt he should try to make a career and at the same time shoulder the wider responsibilities of an adult citizen. We decided to sell up without regrets for our year. We sold well to a man we called "a sucker from the prairies"; packed up and returned to other work and other adventures — including fishing.

CHAPTER FIVE

The Gander River

G ANDER River, Newfoundland. I wish so much I had the ability to describe it in words so that my readers could build a mental picture of this fascinating river. My inadequacy to do this is because I know no words of mine could bring to life the fascinating mystique of its thirty mile length where salmon average only four pounds and where you talk a lot about the exceptional ten pounder. Yet of all rivers in every part of the world which I have been lucky enough to fish, this Gander has stolen my heart. In attempting to give a description of the Gander I had better start by being factual. The river flows out of the great Gander Lake, twenty miles long and maybe five miles and more across at some points. From the estuary entrance at Gander Bay the fish run up into the lake where they disappear in this great sheet of water. Far away on the other side of the lake I am told there are rivers flowing down from the distant hills which the fish run up to spawn. As the woodland country of those hills is undeveloped and largely unexplored, never could I gain any firm knowledge of this terrain. Once, years ago I did try what I was told was the main river on this western side which ran through a big lumber mill and camp. I fished all day and never saw a thing.

The Gander leaves the lake as a swift running stream, a hundred and fifty yards wide with depth varying from about zero to several feet. It is rocky always above and below the water line, with surges, eddies and here and there a calm swift stream until the next rock breaks up the placidity. Some quarter of a mile below where the river runs out of the lake it passes under the rail and road bridges of Glenwood, a small town on the left bank. Glenwood is reached from Gander Town by a splendid paved highway bound for the town of Grand Falls. In 1947 on my first trip to Newfoundland there was no road at all between Gander and Glenwood, a distance of about eighteen miles. We went by a little narrow gauge diesel engined train on a line used mainly for freighting lumber. Gander was then just a small settlement of some two hundred people centred almost entirely on the airport whose chief purpose was to act as a refuelling staging post for trans-Atlantic aircraft bound for Montreal or New York, or to Europe on the return journey. In those early post-war years airlines had not the range to fly non-stop, hence the use of Gander in war had extended to peace time. As the size and range of more modern types were developed ousting the older Constellations and Boeing Stratocruisers, non-stop flying became a normal operation with Gander over-flown. I thought, entirely wrongly as later events showed, that Gander Airport would be an almost total post-war loss. In the event, Gander Airport today is a thriving busy air centre. Newfoundland has developed a large tourist traffic. In Gander Town where there used to be one rather scruffy inn-cum-eating house, today there are at least eight modern motels: where there used to be a few not very impressive stores, today there is an extremely fine shopping centre: streets of neat frame houses: a road system of city roads with intersections controlled by traffic lights: a large new hospital building and a population that has risen to nearly eight thousand. Today Gander is an important residential and tourist base with an increasing number of industrial plants to add to this transformation from a small fairly primitive collection of buildings of thirty years ago.

In 1947 I arrived in a Boeing Stratocruiser in which passengers could enjoy (if the noise allowed) a curtained lie-down sleeper bunk like those in American trains. The old Stratocruiser had four piston type engines. One of the four seemed frequently to give trouble so the pilots used to boast "that the Stratocruiser was the best three-engined aircraft on the Atlantic".

Arriving at Glenwood off the little diesel train the township looked very much then as it does today. Whereas Gander has been transformed, Glenwood, except for some filling stations and a few more wooden frame houses, is very little changed. It is at Glenwood you meet your guide and canoe to start the down river run to whichever fishing camp you are bound for. In these days canoes have powerful 20 h.p. outboard motors. In 1947 all we had was only a 8 h.p. engine. On moving off from point of embarkation the first manoeuvre the guide does is to swing across the river from left to right bank where he will pick up the narrow deep canoe channel which turns and twists all over the river. Almost at once you shoot under the bridges of the railway and the Gander-Grand Falls highway. Here and for the next few miles downstream the river averages a width of around a hundred yards, but the channel deep enough to keep the canoe off the rocks has to be followed accurately by the guide, skilled in his handling from years of experience on the river. Only someone like this could get you downstream without crashing the canoe against rocks seen and others hidden just below the surface of these turbulent waters. For half a mile below Glenwood there is the good sight of fishermen either standing on, or behind almost every rock. These are the local sportsmen who each evening wade out to their favourite perches and, having got position, patiently cast out their lines. When fish are running the reward of patience is odds on that during the evening each of the fishermen will get hold of at least one and probably more salmon.

In Newfoundland all fishing is free subject to a Provincial Licence and no fish caught by rod and line is allowed to be sold so each of those happy sportsmen is clinging around or on some rock just for the fun of it. On a good day of running fish I am told that sixty salmon have been reported as one evening's catch. After this half mile below Glenwood the river widens: the rocky swirling water gives way to a comparatively calm stretch but this peaceful progress is a delusion. Ahead the river narrows and a quarter of a mile below a bar of broken white water covers the whole width. We zig-zag on course through the calm then our bows hit the beginning of the angry water which marks the start of the fiercest rapids of the thirty mile length. We shoot on down at a terrifying pace. We twist and turn on our course and here it is the guide's skill that we completely depend on not to go crashing into some mid-stream rock. The front half of the canoe rears high on the crest of a wave then is slammed down as the stern takes on this challenge of stability and controllability. The canoe and our guide win this big one and a dozen smaller before we have finished shooting rapids. Throughout it all our guide is quite unperturbed by the water turmoil boiling around us. In the reverse way, coming up stream on the journey back to Glenwood guides land their passengers on the bank below the rapids, picking them up again after he has taken the canoe under full engine power through waves and broken water which, until one has seen it happen, look impossible to drive through. Since, many years ago, a canoe capsized and one passenger was drowned, anyone who really insists on being allowed to make this passage has to put on a life-saving jacket. The other rapids to be gone through seem like child's play after the big falls. The next five miles or so is pleasant going with thick wooded banks of pine and fir. A watering stag looks up, stares at the canoe and quite unworried by such a strange sight, turns round to retreat gently into the backwoods. Occasionally we pass another moored canoe with a lone fisherman standing in the bows casting into the top of some likely run. We call or signal "What luck"? and feel optimistically excited for ourselves when a positive answer comes back.

Now, ahead we see a great lake, maybe four miles long and two broad. This is Fourth Pond. To me the word "pond" has meant at home a little circle of water, usually somewhere near the farmyard. Not so in Newfoundland. Gander River has four of these ponds or lakes in its length. A few miles above Gander Bay there is First Pond with its famous fishing just above First Pond Bar where the river runs out of the Pond. Here more salmon are caught than in any other one spot. All the visitor needs is to rent a guide and canoe for the day. If his guide is keen and clever in his choice of mooring spot he anchors the canoe and stays put all day with his angler casting out into the stream, hoping to hook a resting fish or one as it crosses the bar on the way up-river. Now there is a road from Gander to Gander Bay, First Pond Bar is easy to reach. In the old days to fish First Pond Bar meant a three-hour trip downstream from Glenwood and a longer return time against the current. Today anyone with a canoe can easily get a full day's fishing based on Gander Town or stay at one of the several fishing camps on the water's edge. On a fine Saturday or Sunday, for Sunday fishing is allowed, in the fish running season, you may find thirty or forty canoes spaced across the length of the sand bar. Your guide needs to be up early to make sure of a good canoe position for visitors to the camps come from all over Canada and the States. Quite a few can be seen lying back in the canoe smoking a big cigar while the guide takes on the duty of flogging the water hour after hour until a fish is hooked when the rod is handed over to the visitor. This may not be quite my idea of fishing but it works and gives a lot of pleasure to a lot of people.

In fishing gossip about the river the four Ponds are always used by locals to identify a particular place like: "Just above Third Pond we lost it", or "Halfway between Third and Fourth we hooked that big fish". The four great sheets of water are so shallow that to get through the guide must know the narrow twisting navigable passage clear of hidden rocks, timber logs and sand bars. The Ponds are about four or five miles long but there is no fishing in them, for the salmon just run straight through. After First Pond, going upstream, there are only few fishing places, but after Second Pond and short of Third Pond there are five miles of good fishable broken water leading to "Forces Rattle"; "Rattle" being the local word for rapids. "Forces Rattle" is the happy fishing ground for fishermen from the "Allied Camp", a beautifully located luxurious camp, with a dozen or so guides in smart grey uniforms, owned and run by aviation industrial chiefs. Their guests are flown in from Gander Airport by helicopter or seaplane for a week's fishing. Airline executives and airline pilots make up the guest lists. Passing upstream from the Allied Camp and Forces Rattle you come to Third Pond. At the head of the Pond the stream runs alongside the right bank in a 20-yard wide channel about 200 yards in length. "Jordans" is the name of this pool which ranks second best to First Pond Bar. A dozen canoes may be anchored here. Again the Havana aroma; the reclining cushion, the guide casting with an almost mechanical rhythm until, suddenly a fish is hooked. The Havana is cast overboard: the lumbering shape sits up; the rod is placed in his hand and he starts his $100 a day's worth of sport.

"Jordans" is a meeting point for Allied canoes from downstream and canoes from the upstream camps. Here it is to some extent competitive fishing, being a case of who gets there early enough to anchor at one of the thought-to-be most likely prospects for hooking a fish.

From Jordans upstream the river is at least a third of a mile wide, but broken up by two thickly wooded islands. The current may be slow but everywhere jagged rocks point their noses up through the water and the navigable channel is often only just wide enough to take a canoe. Here in this next half mile there must be a dozen or more places well known to the guides where the fish lie. The guides know with great accuracy which of these will hold fish at any particular water level. Half a mile up from Jordans you come to "Joe Batts" pool. Here, hidden in the trees, are the remains of the old Government camp, its one main building of three rooms with a small guide's sleeping hut hard by, now deserted and falling to bits. It was to this camp my wife and I came in 1947 as guests of the Newfoundland Provincial Government Fishing Department. Today the Newfoundland Government have a fine smart modern camp some miles up at the head of Fourth Pond. Go another mile and a half upstream from Joe Batts and, standing high on a rocky cliff on the left bank is the camp which has become for me my Gander River home for something like the last twenty summers.

In my first years on the river this camp belonged to the Anglo-Newfoundland Development Company with its vast timber areas, the paper mill at Grand Falls and also the formidable Edwardian stone mansion built by Lord Northcliffe for himself and his visiting guests. His nephew, the present Lord Rothermere, succeeded to the position of major shareholder in the company and it was through his kindness that I made my first of many visits to his camp. In due course the A.N.D. Company was merged with another great Canadian paper company, Price Bros., and still later Price Bros. was taken over by the Abitibi Paper and Mining Group; the present owners. On my first visit to the A.N.D. Camp I was lucky enough to have been put in the care of Walter Tucker, a real and true friend, as fine a fisherman as I have ever met. Over the years Walter and I have talked and talked fishing. We would have bored the pants off anyone who was not of our tribe. "Fishing greased line in fast water. Do you strike or do you let the fish take slack and hook itself?" "Does fly colour really matter or is it fly size that counts?" "Your fish rises and misses." "Do you rest him or give it another chance at once?" There are those and dozens of other unanswered arguable questions that have kept a fisherman happy covering many an evening and many a drink. Walter combined his duties as an executive of the paper company with being for several years Mayor of Grand Falls. He now has retired from his executive post but, happily for all, Walter continues to look after the fishings and the fishing camps on the Gander and on the Hunt River up in Labrador, which are kept for the company's customer-guests. In another part of this book I have described my visit in 1974 to this famous Hunt River.

From A.N.D. Camp, on its rock summit you look down on to

the Home Pool. The camp is a single storey bungalow type. A long fly-proofed verandah runs the whole length of the front of the building. Here you can dump your gear in one corner, relax in an easy chair and watch for fish showing in the Home Pool below. From this verandah I can never tire of seeing the sunsets over forest and water. I have watched a whole herd of deer crossing in line the shallows. I have been disturbed just as it gets dark by a crash in the back regions. There, rummaging in the refuse tip, was a little black bear which had to be chased off by one of the guides. Inside the bungalow, the main living room with its log burning stove capable of transforming shivers into sweating heat and in an astonishingly short time. At the far end of the living room is the dining section. One table with eight chairs and a cupboard full of lovely bottles. A big fridge so that the drink can always be cold. The kitchen leading off with an extension the far end for the guides' dining room. Leading off the living room, two little rooms each with two beds, and one with a single bed. Each has its very small basin of running water, like in one of our railway sleepers. No cupboards. Just a few clothes hangers for in the camp you need nothing beyond pants, shirt and coat. The glory is in throwing off your clothes at night, going to the little shower and lavatory room: cleaning up: get between blankets and you are off until morning — when you wake up and put on the same clothes you threw off last night. Electric light, water heating, lots of ice are the luxuries given off by the camp's own diesel powered generating system. Usual camp routine: breakfast 8 a.m., off in your canoe to some spot agreed with your guide as being a likely bet. Back at noon for "dinner". Sleep till 4 p.m. then out again until six or so. Back for drinks and food while the guides have their supper, then off again until nine or nine thirty when the light is failing and you are ready for a shower and bed. For me the day starts at 5.30 to 6 a.m. and for me it is the best and most exciting hour. Quickly I pull on last night's trousers and shirt then treading oh so softly, opening doors oh so gently so as not to disturb the other sleepers I leave my little single room. On the verandah I put on my long waders, spray my hat, arms and neck with anti-fly lotion, put a box of flies, nylon and scissors in jacket pocket and I am ready. On a rack underneath the pillars supporting the bungalow rods are laid. I pull out my little 9' greenheart spliced rod, check the nylon leader, approve of the No. 7 black single hook moose hair fly already on the cast and down the steps to the water's edge. I know so well every underwater rock of that pool that I feel I could wade down it blindfold. I start at the top of the stream with a short line. Below me about seventy yards of water which broadens out towards the tail. At first I am only up to my knees in water. By the end of the pool where it becomes a deep wide stream with not enough current to carry a fly, I am as deep as I can go in full waders. As I start down the pool I see two fish below me. So I know new fish are here this morning. A quarter way down I feel a pull. No rise seen. For a few seconds I think it is one of the ¼ or ½ cutthroat trout. Then I feel the pull again. I strike to get the fly home in the fish's mouth. The next moment the reel screams. The line runs out to the backing and a lovely fresh fish of 5 lbs throws itself into the air. Alas: for all my care and hopes the fly comes back. He is gone. During the jump, even though I lowered the tip of the rod, he got rid of the fly as he leapt. One asks oneself the eternal lost fish questions. "Was it my fault?" This time I feel I can honestly return a verdict of "Not Guilty". No purpose in changing fly so down the pool I work, fishing it literally foot by foot. About two-thirds down a beautiful rise on the far side of the stream. He never touched it so I rest him, and myself, for five minutes. I start well above where he rose and fish that ten yards with infinite care. Exactly the same cast to the same spot and again he comes up. This time he meant business and hooked himself well and truly. Twice he took half the backing out. Several jumps feet clear of the water then he began to tire. Stepping slowly carefully backwards to avoid tripping I bring him to the shallow water on a short line. When I have him quite beat and lying on his side on top of the water I walk him back until he slides out on to the gentle grass edge. He is safely beached and weighs just on 5 lbs. By now it is 7.30 a.m. and other guests in their pyjamas had watched from the verandah the reward of early rising. Waders off. Hot coffee and the day has started well.

Above our camp was about three miles of excellent water. If any Gander fishermen read this the names: Dark Angle, Pine Tree, Green Lawn: The Shute, Fourth Pond Outlet; all will mean for them happy memories. Each one of these pools varies in character. Each must be fished in a different way. I know the Gander fish can be labelled small compared with other rivers but show me another where you may rise the same fish six times then, after changing size and dressing of the fly maybe three or four times, you finally get him to take properly.

On our first visit to the Gander, things were very different from today. To begin with, once past Glenwood we never saw another canoe. By 1954 fishing camps had been established so that, what with no road to Gander Bay, there was regular river traffic up and down in a fairly steady stream. In an hour there might be a dozen canoes past our camp and through the Home Pool. One good result of the opening of the Gander-Gander Bay road is that river traffic is now drastically reduced; First Pond Bar can be walked easily from the highway while trucks carry freight that previously had to go by water. Our 1947 canoe had such a low powered motor that coming up against current the guide often had to resort to poling which made trips slow and tedious.

That first 1947 visit was to fulfil a commission from the first Lord Kemsley to write an article for the *Sunday Times* on terms so generous as to cover and more my costs. I had suggested to him the exploration of the Gander following a report I had received on its undeveloped fishing potential. In due course the article appeared under the title "An Angler's Paradise". My wife and I stayed at the now derelict Government camp I have already described off Joe Batts' Pool. Two rooms; kitchen; no water—hot or cold; outside privy. One Government guide who cooked and fished with us. Alas, this excellent fellow, of considerable age even then, was over-thirsty. Later he become Senior Warden on the river, but being very over-thirsty on good Scotch one evening he fell overboard from his canoe and was drowned. Our first few days were blank for the fish were not up yet. However, the next three days were good. I scarcely had to go beyond Joe Batts, the pool opposite the camp which I could wade easily. I had all the fun I needed and I forget now how many salmon I managed to beach.

It was 1959 that I did my second and last trip to an improved but still fairly primitive Government Camp, still on the same spot for it was not until the next year that the Government moved to its smart new camp at the end of Fourth Pond. I had as companion Antony (now Sir Antony) and Freda Milward. Tony, friend and colleague on the Board of B.E.A. and Freda were both good and keen fishers and I could not have wished for a better couple to share the camp. Now we had a cleared pathway to a twin outdoor privy with "Ladies" painted on one door and "Gents" on the other, so we felt we were making progress in essential amenities. In six days I had fifteen to my rod and several more hooked and lost. This sounds not a big catch but the water was low and dozens of others risen, one seven times. The sun blazed down and we fished stripped to the waist. The day I remember best was when we started early in the morning to make a carefully planned strategic raid on Forces Rattle, below Third Pond which by then had become the almost recognized preserve of the Allied Camp canoes. *The Field* published an article I wrote called "Going back to Gander" and I reproduce here that particular part of my article which described the Forces Rattle Raid:

> By nine the party is ready in four canoes with lunch on board to leave for a raid on the Forces Rattle rapids, about 50 minutes downstream through Third Pond and a couple of miles below the Allied Camp. This raid of ours on the favourite Allied ground is strategically planned and cunningly timed, for the evening before we had watched the Allied canoe fleet progressing up to Glenwood to collect stores and bring down a new batch of their guests. We calculated — and rightly — that for most of the day we should have the place to ourselves. I settle to try the top of a smooth glide above the rapids. The guide anchors the canoe and, with a Moose Hair and greased line, I begin with a short cast.
>
> Almost at once I rise a fish. He comes short and is shy of a second go. Ten minutes blank and we drop down some 15 yards. I see T. is into a good fish, which, with rod bent double, he works up from the head of the falls. After 20 minutes, I see with joy tinged with slight envy the fish safely netted.
>
> We decide to go down into the rapids. I start casting in the fast rocky stream. Suddenly I am taken with a bang and the tussle commences. The line slackens. The fly comes back and he is away — victory to the fish. However, luck turns and by lunch I have two and the others three. Picnic on the shore and then a bathe in warm river water. Afterwards we motor slowly back, fishing likely places but without result. Camp at 3 p.m. and sleep till six and our evening high tea.

After this 1959 trip I was lucky enough to transfer my base to the A.N.D. Camp for an annual week's visit, and this largely due to my good friend Bob Morrow, Q.C., D.F.L., a distinguished R.C.A.F. fighter-pilot, Queen's Counsel in Quebec Province and then a director of Price Brothers, now my hosts. With Bob in the camp it was always a case of laughter and fishing, then more laughter and more fishing. I caught and entered in the fishing book for the Gander, a heavy fish of 10 lbs 3 oz. My entry was just above one by Bob who had the day before also got a big one turning the scale of 10 lbs 1 oz. Of course, I boasted of my fish over his poor little one when compared to mine, which up to then held the season's record. Bob denied the accuracy of my weight. I brought the guide in as my witness at the weighing. I was accused of putting pebbles down its gullet to boost the scale reading. This I hotly denied. The argument went on, and so did the accompanying whisky, for most of that evening. I went to bed confident of victory. Next morning to my horror and disgust I found the "1" of Bob's writing had been made into a neat figure "4". I was powerless in my defeat by such dishonest monstrous means: but there it was, and typical of the gay fun we had (but I forget: I must not now use that good descriptive word any more).

On my last visit in 1975 Gander conditions were the worst within memory of the guides. The water level was so low that we could not get up or down without manhandling of the canoe. Finally the camp had to be closed until rain came. In my week, by working really hard, I managed to get just four fish.

During the summer of 1976 I could not get to the Gander. Instead I took a nephew to the Restigouche River in New Brunswick and in another part of this book I give some description of our experiences on that famous river. Meanwhile my hope was that in 1977 I might find myself once again wading the Home Pool at dawn. I love so much this Gander River of happiness for all who float down its stream and cast into its waters.

My Gander hopes were fulfilled. July 1977 and I was back there for the best season ever. Read my last chapter and you will see just how and why.

CHAPTER SIX

Labrador

L ABRADOR where the dogs come from, and the salmon —
but not for me.

For years I had heard of the two wonderful rivers, Eagle and
Hunt. I expect there are lots of others but it is of these two that
I had heard. For years I had hoped that luck would be such
that I should be asked as a guest to one or the other. The Eagle
has on its banks the camp of the Royal Canadian Air Force.
Here senior members of the R.C.A.F. and other N.A.T.O. Air
Forces are flown in by R.C.A.F. weekly service. Here, I am
reliably told, you just cannot help hooking, or anyhow rising, a
huge number of fish each day. It is, like the Gander, a grilse
river with average weight of around 5 lbs. Maybe in the war,
when I had a lot to do with the R.C.A.F. and its Ministers over
the Commonwealth Air Training plan, I might have qualified
for an invitation but in those days firstly we were all too busy
and secondly the camp is a post-war enterprise. Now I can
think of no earthly reason why I should ever be invited. But
with the Hunt River I have been more lucky. Bob Morrow, the
good friend I write about in my Gander River description, said
that as a Director of Price Bros. he would be delighted to take
me up to their camp on the Hunt for six days fishing. The fish
here, he promised me, were no grilse. A 20 pounder would be
expected. Under good conditions I could expect what? Four,
six, eight, ten fish in a day. My rod would be bent all the time,
nearly. Just time to take a fish out of the net, untie the fly, cast
out again and I would be into another. This was the prospect I
had in my mind when I landed at Montreal in the last week of
July 1974. I was to stay with Bob and his lovely charming wife,
Connie, at their house on the St Bruno Golf Club estate about
twenty miles south of the city across the St Lawrence, and we
were to fly to Labrador the next day.

It was afternoon in Montreal when we landed so our motor
drive from Dorval Airport was made in the rush hour. The

33

packed highway pattern with its countless intersections and loops makes Spaghetti Junction look like a straight line. The weather was hot; the swimming pool heaven, the iced drinks superb. My rods and tackle were in the hall ready for next morning. I was tingling with excitement. The plan was to fly up in the Price Bros. private Lear jet direct to Goose Bay. The trip would take about three hours. Fellow passengers would be fellow fishermen guests in the Camp. There was "Cope", a great man from across the U.S.A. border with business in Illinois, a splendid character from New York, call him Steve, Bob and myself. Like so many flight plans for non-scheduled operations, our take-off at 9.30 a.m. finally meant 11 a.m. because Steve's plane from N.Y. came in late. Private jet travel is just something. Highly competent and delightful captain and second pilot; a very lovely girl as stewardess in Price Bros. smart grey uniform. Open bar with so many, too many, iced drinks displayed before the thirsty. Thirty thousand feet up in bright sunshine with a white cloud carpet below us. Small wonder that the three hours just swept by. Goose Bay, which I had been in and out of so many times during the War, had not altered much. The airport runways border the sea inlet so they can operate both land aircraft or seaplanes from the field. As a N.A.T.O. base the life of the small community consists mainly of Service personnel and their families. Air Canada and Provincial Airways both run services from Montreal and Quebec to Goose and to Gander, Newfoundland. There is a large Military and Civil Hospital — which we were to be thankful for later on. Our Lear jet shot off back either to Montreal or New York, and we four clambered into a wheel and float eight seater high wing single engine De Havilland "Otter". This is about the most successful and useful aerial cart-horse used in the wilds of Canada. The trip to the landing water at the mouth of the Hunt River was about 160 miles north and should take around one and a half hours.

I took the second pilot's seat up in front to get a fine view of the flat deserted, timbered country intersected by innumerable steams and lakes. On my right quarter was the Polar Sea. We followed the coast but flying direct over such an irregular coast line sometimes we found ourselves several miles inland and sometimes well out to sea. An hour and a quarter out and I was starting to look for the entrance to the Hunt River on the large scale map. Then out to sea, to my astonishment, I saw on the horizon, but drawing closer as we flew on, what looked like a long line of cliffs; the white cliffs of Dover. I asked our pilot what was I seeing. "That," he said, "Oh, that's the iceflow." As the weather becomes warmer this gigantic mass drifts slowly south melting all the time. Below I spotted the Hunt estuary with its sheet of smooth water on which we would be landing in a few minutes. Far below I could see four canoes which had come down to take us up to the Camp four miles upstream.

London yesterday. Northern Labrador today. London-Montreal-Goose and now a hundred and fifty miles into the blue. How many thousands of miles I did not know, but only that it was quite a long way. Well worth it, I felt, for the fishing I was going to enjoy. We landed. The seaplane was moored. We stepped down on to the floats. The canoes came alongside.

"Well, what's the fishing like?" shouted Bob. Back came a sad voice, "There isn't a fish in the river". Complete silence. I was stunned and I guess the others were too. Then we heard the explanation of this awful news. The White Cliffs of Dover: the ice flow was late by at least a week in dissolving. Not a salmon could or would pass under the deep base of the icebergs forming this continuous barrage. I did feel a bit shattered at this, the end of my hopes and at the end of such a long, long journey. However, there was nothing either to be said or done. I got some comfort when I was told that sea trout were unaffected by the ice blockage and some were up the river already. I did not know then how good this sea trout fishing was to turn out as compensation for no salmon.

The Camp was in the form of a square frame wooden building not unlike the Gander Camp. Central living room with one end for meals and a very fine wood burning stove and three double bunk rooms. Shower and loo. All electric lit from the Camp plant. The fly proofing was closer than in Newfoundland. The rules about being careful never to forget to use the double doors, one ordinary and the other a flyproof protection were of vital importance if the black flies, of which on the Gander there were none, were to be kept out. We were issued with cloth headmasks leaving just two slits for eyes and gauntlet gloves to protect hands, wrists and arms for without all the protective clothing fishing would have been impossible in the mornings or evenings. That first evening we unpacked, fixed gear, had supper and early bed. Next morning after breakfast the canoes went half a mile upstream to just below a good fast run. I mounted a No. 7 Black Moose and started to cast out. Within minutes I rose a fish which I thought must be a salmon the way it tore off line and let me feel its strength. It jumped and I saw it was no salmon but a magnificent sea trout. After a real struggle my guide netted it. Six pounds. That morning I had two more and lost two or three. I will not weary readers with any story of each fish caught. Sufficient to say that in two days we had become so blasé that anything under about three pounds we unhooked and put back in the river. Never before or since have I had such marvellous sea trout fishing on light tackle and a little 9′ 6″ split-cane fly rod. It was after dinner on the third evening that disaster hit us. Steve had paid visits to the Camp in previous years and was admired and beloved by the Eskimo guides and such of their families as had come to the Camp for his Annual Magic Circle conjuring display. Steve, around seventy years old, had enjoyed a truly varied life. Starting as a penniless American lad doing a newspaper deliver circuit to earn the odd dollars, he was finishing up as a very rich man indeed. Now he was owner of paper mills and newspapers. He and his wife had a New York apartment famed for beautiful period furniture and a fine collection of impressionist paintings. Yet with all this, the exercise of his art, skill and knowledge as a great illusionist and conjuror still gave him greater pleasure than his many other successes in different directions. Steve had taken up magic as a young man and had got to the very top of his profession. In his day he could command staggeringly large fees in London, Paris, New York and as many of the world's capitals as he chose to visit. When he turned his talents to commerce he had kept in magic practice for his own enjoyment and that of his friends. Never could a 5 cent piece disappear more convincingly before your eyes to re-appear in your right ear; never could a card pack be better shuffled than by me but when the pack was dealt somehow it was I who got the two's and three's and Steve the four aces, four kings and one queen. In his life he had three loves. First, his wife who became tragically ill and died. Secondly, Sir Winston Churchill who Steve had entertained in his home during Churchill's after war visits to New York. Thirdly, fishing. And a first-class fisherman he was.

Once every year Eskimos and their families came in to the Camp to see Steve go through a repertoire of tricks that kept not only the Eskimos amazed but fellow guests as well. On this particular evening the show was to be after dinner. Before dinner we sat round the table having highballs. Steve was leaning back in an upright dining room chair. At the particular moment he was gesticulating with one arm to emphasize some point of a story. There was one almighty crash as Steve overbalanced backwards. He lay motionless. We rushed to pick him up. It took three of us to lift his heavy limp frame on to the sofa. Terribly white, he managed to murmur — "I think I'm all right". But we only had to look at him to know this was far from true. He complained of great pain in chest and side. We got him on to this bed, managed to get his clothes off and gave a hot bottle to stop the shivering from shock. We gave him pain-killing drugs and told him to try to sleep. The three of us then went next door for a conference. Here we were in the wilds, more than 160 miles north of Goose Bay. No telephone. No radio. No doctor. Our seaplane was down at the river mouth. The pilot was in a camp down there. The Otter had radio but until well up to a good height it could not transmit to and receive from Goose Bay control. We decided the only thing to do was to cut out the rest of the trip. Take down rods and pack our gear that evening to make an early start down river next morning. We sent one guide down at dawn to warn the pilot to be ready for take off. Early next morning Steve was feeling better but quite unable to move without agonising pain. We supported him to one of the canoes, getting him into the easiest position we could find for him. When we got alongside the Otter, he was hoisted through the door and laid down on the floor. We took off and climbed to 7,000 feet. The pilot got Goose on the R.T. and explained. Goose promised that a doctor and ambulance would be standing by as we landed. Poor Steve was put on a stretcher, whirled off to the hospital, x-rayed and found to have various ribs fractured and severe skin bruising. Bob Morrow from the Otter R.T. had whistled up the Lear jet from Montreal to land at Goose around early afternoon. It would pick up Steve and fly him direct to New York where he could go straight into his favourite hospital. I hesitate to think what our little expedition must, in total, have cost our kind and generous hosts. For myself: there I was at Goose but not stranded for once the radio had been free of Steve's worries and cares, I too had been busy. Price Bros.' representative at Goose to Walter Tucker of Price Bros. in

Grand Falls, Newfoundland and please could Lord B. arrive that afternoon in Gander and would there be room for him—it was midweek—in the camp for 3 days. Also please to book a seat on Provincial Airways' afternoon service from Goose to Gander. Dear Walter just fixed the lot. Around 5 p.m. the plane landed at Gander and Walter was there to meet me. No, there was no one in the Camp before Saturday. Yes, Walter would come down river with me. Yes, two guides had been organised at Glenwood and were even now waiting for us. Camp by 7 p.m. Drink by 7.05 p.m. Food and, believe it or not, a lovely fish from the Home Pool by 9 p.m.

For me it was a case of "Goodbye Labrador—Newfoundland here I come."

CHAPTER SEVEN

Trips to the Restigouche

BUY a Rolls-Royce and it is generally accepted you have about the best. Fish the Restigouche River in New Brunswick, Canada and it is generally accepted that you are on about the best salmon river in Eastern Canada. I don't see myself ever in the position to buy a Rolls-Royce but I have been extraordinarily lucky to have fished the Restigouche for three summers.

On my first trip I found myself in Fredericton, New Brunswick, about to fly some 150 miles "into the blue" to the fishing camp belonging to Mr K. C. Irving whose guest I was to be.

Lytton Strachey looking at the Albert Hall and the Albert Memorial said he felt that "the Spirit of the Prince Consort brooded o'er the land". So in Fredericton I felt the spirit of Lord Beaverbrook brooded o'er that city. I walked into the "Lord Beaverbrook", the leading hotel. Just down the main street I came to a statue of Lord Beaverbrook erected by public subscription. Next call was to the Beaverbrook Art Gallery. Freely do I admit I know next to nothing about pictures but even to my untrained eyes it was a very mixed lot. It is not for me to pontificate when profusion becomes confusion. A Salvador Dali, 14 feet high, 10 feet wide dominated a main gallery wall. Gainsborough's "Peasant Girl Gathering Faggots", Graham Sutherland's several paintings of Lord Beaverbrook and four of his sketches of Mr Churchill, which he disliked so very much; a "Drinking Party at Norwich" by Mercier painted in 1750. Hard by was the Canadian War Memorial's Collection, and works of young Canadian artists in oils, water colours and crayon. My brain was quite incapable of digesting this quick change variety described at the Opening of the Gallery in 1959 by the Art Historian, Doctor W. G. Constable of U.S.A., as "An incomparable gift to the Arts in Canada", and certainly visitors flock to Fredericton from all parts of Canada. The

Gallery was part of the 10 million dollars Lord Beaverbrook's biographer A. J. P. Taylor reckons he gave to the State of New Brunswick during his lifetime. A good wad of the remainder must have been swallowed up in help to the University of New Brunswick, at Fredericton, of which Lord Beaverbrook became the first Chancellor in 1947. "The Lady Beaverbrook residential home for men"; a gymnasium; a variety of student scholarships and the setting up of the Beaverbrook Foundation are some of the gifts of this remarkable man who, in his home town, was, and still is rightly regarded as their greatest benefactor ever.

My host, K. C. Irving, to whose fishing camp I was on my way, comes into the same category of success men from the Maritimes as Lord Beaverbrook. He is the millionaire, self-made since the end of the First World War, who now owns two million acres of forest land, an oil empire ranging from a fleet of tankers, storage and refining plants, down to Irving petrol pumps at 3,000 Irving service stations to be found all through the Maritimes; pump and paper mills, a few mines, a whole lot of newspapers, yet he still lives simply, makes his own bed and cleans his own shoes. I bet not many of our millionaires do that!

K. C. Irving has given up fishing yet has 26 miles of the Restigouche and two splendidly equipped fishing camps for his family, his friends and business associates. He is too busy to fish and when he does pay one of his fleeting visits to a fishing camp he can't wait not to get on the river, but into the forest to see how fare his nursery plantations of young trees for here is the love that transcends all his many other interests. The romantic rise of this man from small beginnings has yet to be written. In 1919 a garage, then the local Ford Motor franchise, which in turn led to the foundation of his oil empire: two gasoline filling stations, one 350 gallon tank truck and oil from Oklahoma which soon met with opposition from the oil giants. These early years saw the truly cheeky challenge to the great Imperial Oil Company by a young man who this giant concern was determined to squash when he declined to comply and come to heel. From these beginnings the Irving empire has steadily expanded to such a size that I doubt if he, himself, knows the details of its full extent. In charitable gifts and foundations he has not tried to emulate his friend Lord Beaverbrook's generosity. Once he said to me, "If I don't give great sums to charity it is because I use my money to give employment". He told me this apropos of the story of the taking over in 1950 of an outmoded shipbuilding and dry dock company. There were 200 men employed and all fearful of their future in a decaying concern. Today this company employs 1,500 men and builds ships up to 30,000 tons. A bankrupt paper mill was rescued. Today the mill has 150 men and turns out 200 tons daily of its particular paper. With this growth of the Irving empire must go need for quick communications for himself, his three sons who now divide the running — one the timber forest and the pulp and paper mills; another the oil interests and the third the mines and the newspapers. Hence the fleet of Irving aircraft in one of which I was to fly to the camp that evening. There are several executive aircraft, and a Jet Ranger Helicopter has been added. As well as executive aircraft there are a number of wartime type of U.S.A. single seaters, equipped as water tank carriers called out as soon as any forest fire has broken out to drop thousands of gallons. A closer, more united family than these Irvings it would be hard to find. My sole criticism is that father and sons never seem to stop working. Though I know they do sometimes get away with their wives and children and I can only conclude that in the success and ceaseless expansion of the empire they find reward and happiness. In business K.C. has the reputation of a man of his word, but tough and rough, if need be. Personally to me as his guest, I find him gentle, so modest and kind.

That evening we took off for the camp landing strip. We flew for an hour and a half over one vast forest. Sometimes the forest was intersected by a straight road or single track railway line, so far as the eye could see coming from nowhere and going nowhere. Lakes and an occasional river passed by below. In the distance ahead I saw a range of hills. These hills, our pilot told me, give the answer as to whether we can make the landing strip or have to retreat back to Fredericton. If the hills are clear of cloud and fog the aircraft can get in safely to the camp strip. Sometimes in a spell of bad weather air communication to the camp can be cut for days on end. For us the weather was kind and we made it easily and safely. Since then the original gravel strip has become a fully fledged private airport with hard runway, control tower with R.T., hangars, a workshop and never less than three or four Irving insignia-bearing aircraft on the apron. My first morning I was woken early by the roar of a low flying aircraft which seemed to be flying backwards and forwards over my head. This, I learnt, was the regular morning operation of spraying the camp with D.D.T. against flies and mosquitos. After spraying our camp, it flew off to do the same spraying job over Irving lumber camps spread about the forest. Small wonder that while some of the paper companies had trouble getting and holding their labour force the Irving camps had no such difficulty.

The camp consisted of the centre block; a living room with a huge open fireplace, with dining alcove leading to a completely modern equipped kitchen, manned by a chef and two University students on their summer vacation work. Off the centre block were two passages leading to the twelve bedrooms each with its own bathroom. Electric light came from the camp diesel plant which also looked after the refrigeration and hot water system. If air communications were cancelled due to weather the outer world could be reached by a radio telephone system of three channels; one for oil interests, one for timber and the third for general use, including even the booking for me of air reservations for my return to the U.K. All in all, it was a pretty complete outfit of great comfort for those lucky enough to be K.C.'s guests.

We had about twenty-six miles of river to fish. Each guest was allotted a guide with outboard engined canoe. The first morning my guide motored me downstream for several miles to show me a bit of the river and some of the pools. The weather was hot and the water so clear that on our passage as we passed through a pool we could count the salmon and grilse lying there. As far upstream as our camp the river was not big, about the breadth of the middle reaches of the Spey or Dee. This lovely river ran through forest down to the river banks. It was a fisherman's dream and winding with every sort of pool; sometimes shallow, rocky and fast, other times just a graceful gentle current and occasionally a deep length of water when the bottom was too far down to see clearly what the pool held. We came to a pool the guide said we must try. About forty yards long, it ran straight and smooth. At the head of the pool the engine was cut and we drifted down the centre, silently and motionless. At the canoe's bows the guide knelt and counted out to me the fish he could see: "Two very big fish behind one rock", several he judged of about twelve pounds and towards the tail of the pool where the water shallowed a school of grilse.

Under the lee of the bank very carefully and gently the guide poled us up to the head of the pool. We were to have a go at the two big fish we had seen. I tied a small No. 7 Black Moose hair fly on to a 12-lb breaking strain leader. I waded into the water as far as I dared without disturbing the pool. It was a long cast with my little single-handed Sharp of Aberdeen's spliced ten foot greenheart and a white floating line. No one in Canada uses anything except a single-handed rod. I believe that if anyone produced one of our two-handed he would be thought a bit mental or laughed off the river. My first cast covered the water where the two fish lay. My guide reported no move. I cast again. "He moved that time," said the guide. I cast again. "Look out, he's coming for it." Even as he spoke there was a swirl and the flat surface of the water was broken. I felt him pull and at once gave him line from the loop of slack I had in my left hand. Then I felt the line tighten. I struck and he was on and, I prayed, well hooked. I won't weary readers with an account of how that fish fought. He jumped three or four times. He had all my backing out twice. Sufficient to report he weighed 22 lbs and had taken around the customary lb a minute before he was safely netted. About five o'clock we motored upstream back to the camp with two salmon and two grilse in the canoe. I was tired and thirsty. Then the blow fell. No one, alas, had warned me. The camp was absolutely dry. No liquor of any sort was served. After a long hot day I had been coming up river with my tongue hanging out in expectation of that long well iced gin and tonic.

I learnt, but too late, that my host was a confirmed teetotaller as were all the rest of his family. K.C. told me later that in his youth, which included service as a pilot in the R.A.F. at the end of 1918, he had seen so much trouble and unhappiness caused to men and their families by alcohol that he decided he would have none of it for himself and those around him and that went for his sons too who held similar views. Once over the shock I adapted myself to his custom and for the rest of my visit did my best with iced coca-cola. Good but not quite the same as a good Scotch and soda after a long day.

However, if one accepts a man's hospitality one must accept and respect his wishes. For my two subsequent visits I confess to packing a bottle of Scotch in my luggage and I found I was not the only guest to do this. When we came back to camp each of us would go to his room carrying a tumbler of ice and get the bottle out from the bottom drawer. Not one of us would have dreamt of taking a bottle, or even a glass of liquor into the living room, or even have our bottle conspicuously on the dressing table. This modest private stimulant was, I have reason to believe, known and understood by K.C.

K.C. flew in for one day just to see how we were getting on in camp. He turned not towards the river but was away with his forester to the seedling plantations. "Trees," he said, "are lovely things. They live far longer than any of us and a man can leave them to age as a memorial to his life's work."

At the end of the week with about twelve salmon and a few grilse to my rod I flew back home with an invitation to come again to the camp the following summer and to bring my, then sixteen year-old, daughter. That next summer I came off the Gander River after four days when fish had been scarce and the river too low. At Gander Airport I joined the London-Gander-Halifax Air Canada service to find to my joy Mary Ann sitting comfortably in her seat after a smooth trip across the Atlantic.

We had reservations at the Lord Nelson Hotel in Halifax, Nova Scotia. As we sat in the lounge watching the comings and goings we could have been in Halifax, Yorkshire, or Manchester or Newcastle. A stream of splendid, staid, mostly grey-haired middle aged ladies was coming out from some Women's Conference, Club Meeting, or bun fight. Some had ample busts, some were thin with pince-nez's or steel-rimmed spectacles. All wore frilly flowered hats dressed like the start of a herbaceous border. You find them in the halls and lounges of the leading hotels of provincial cities all over the world. I have seen them in South Africa, in Australia, in U.S.A. and now in Canada. These ladies are the very backbone of social stability. They form the firm rock of life's reasoned middle course with no extreme, right or left. They are a truly noble lot that troop through the lobby from their club consultations. They look not poor but not rich. Just GOOD PEOPLE. In the U.S.A. the proportion of widows at these gatherings is high for the U.S.A. is the country where the widow is often better off with her husband dead than when he is alive. That hard-working high-salaried executive has worked himself to a premature death, often aided by the "office bar" which is cozy, warm and welcoming for the half-hour to spare after the office is shut and before the evening commuters' train leaves Grand Central.

He and his wife have lived comfortably but economically in the knowledge that he carries heavy life assurance. When he dies, at early middle age of stroke or heart, helped on his way by the office bar and the at home week-end highballs, his widow collects. Now she has time as never before to step out. "Daughters of the Empire"; "Daughters of the Revolution"; Women's Clubs, Literary Societies are there to join and be welcomed by other widows in the same now secure circumstances.

Next morning we flew on to the camp, lucky again with the flying weather. The camp was as welcoming and comfortable as before. The same splendid guide for me and one to look after Mary Ann. This time also, there was the joy of one of K.C.'s sons, his charming wife and two children to share with us the camp and river. Alas, the fishing was in contrast to the previous summer. Now the fish were scarce and water level distressingly low. No longer could we drift down a pool counting the salmon. Many of the pools were empty. In others where last year we might have spotted half a dozen fish, now we felt ourselves lucky if we saw one at all. We fished hard. We bathed off the lawns in front of the camp. We relaxed in the sun. I had several blank days but in the week only got three fish. Mary Ann worked hard too but no luck for her. At the end of the week K.C. sent us to Halifax in one of his twin-engined executives and by breakfast next morning we were back home.

Due to various circumstances, and not through lack of kind invitation, there was a gap until 1976 before I could return to the beautiful Restigouche — again as guest of K.C. who was now living for most of the year in Bermuda. The fishing camps had been handed over to his sons and his eldest son, Jim, was to be our host. This time K.C. had kindly said I could bring along a companion. Nephew, David P., was asked and as a 21st birthday present from his parents provided with an economy class return ticket to Halifax. In the event I could not have had a better companion or more fun than with him. David P. is a true and natural fisherman. He makes his own rods, ties his own flies and would go any distance at any time if there was a chance of catching one small trout out of some ditch. By the time I had described to him the camp, the river, the life, he was like a corked up soda bottle bursting with excitement. In spite of advancing years I, too, was in the same state. Due to a

Canadian Air Line dispute our departure was a day later than planned. We landed at Halifax, expecting to see the Irving insignia on one of the planes on the apron. Nothing there. I only knew that we were to be flown to the Irving Airport and thence on to the camp. I did not know where Jim Irving lived. I did not know if K.C. was in Canada or Bermuda. In fact, I was a lost soul who knew nothing. We thought best to reconcile ourselves to no camp flight that night so two pretty weary bodies took themselves in a very expensive, for our limited dollar supply, taxi for the twenty miles run into Halifax city. If our taxi was expensive our driver was splendidly efficient. Halifax hotels, we were told, were sure to be fully booked in this summer holiday season. Our driver had a radio telephone in his car to his head office so as we drove along the six-lane highway, he got busy on the R.T. Just entering the city limits, he turned round in his seat to tell us headquarters had managed to book us into the last two rooms at the Lord Nelson Hotel of my stay with Mary Ann some years before. David and I went to my room and proceeded to get busy on the telephone. By now it was 7 p.m. and every office, Irving or otherwise, was closed. We started on the Irvings in the Halifax telephone directory. Some Irvings answered but not a single replying voice could help us about the particular Irvings we wanted. Next we started long distance on the Irvings at Saint John's, N.S. where I knew K.C. used to have a house. Next we covered the Irvings of Fredericton but again no success. At one moment we did make contact with a K.C. Irving but, alas, it was a different K.C. Clever David finally somehow made a contact who advised us where Jim's home was some hundred miles away. David rang the number given. A voice answered: "Jim Irving here". We explained where we were and what had happened. We learnt we were expected some time but none of our cables of altered plans had been delivered. God moves in mysterious ways to help the weary and beleaguered. Sitting right beside Jim was his Irving pilot who was to fly Jim, Mrs Jim and their daughter out to the camp next morning. Our troubles were over. We were to meet our pilot at 8.30 a.m. next morning at Halifax Airport. He would fly over, pick us up, then fly back to collect the Irving family then all of us would fly to the Irving Airport and thence to the camp. All went well and in spite of Gulf of St Lawrence fog our pilot put us down safely on a strip outside Jim's home. Mrs Jim, their daughter of sixteen, and a friend of theirs who had never caught a salmon got aboard. We talked fishing and the daughter made quite unaffectedly and naturally a classic remark worthy of the Guinness Book of Records: "I've never caught a salmon less than 20 lbs". I fear before our week was over the poor girl had broken her record with several fish of more humble weights. We landed in heavy rain at the Irving Airport I knew so well. We got into cars but to my surprise instead of starting down the road to the camp we went off in the opposite direction. Only then did I learn that we were not bound for the camp I knew but one about an hour and a half run by road upstream. In Canada there is no privately owned water. All belongs to the Provincial Governments who put out to public tender leases for five or ten or more years of stretches of the main salmon rivers. We were to fish several miles of water that K.C. had bid for, and outbid the Restigouche Fishing Club, previous lease holders. When the Club lost their fishings they were left with a white elephant of a camp on the river bank so K.C. negotiated to buy this. It was smaller than his other camp but, again, most comfortable. Centre Block with two living rooms, kitchen and refrigerator. Along its length a verandah overlooking the camp pool. Off one side of the block four twin-bedded rooms each leading into one of two bathrooms, each shared by two bedrooms. We were told that the fishing here, a few miles below Kedgwick town, was better than at the upstream camp. The fish were larger and more of them. As at the other camp David and I were each allotted a guide and canoe. Here the river was considerably bigger but had the same wonderful variety of pools each of different character. The weather was Canadian Summer, the sky was cloudless; the sun hot and a water temperature dangerously near the high point for fishing which I put at 63°F. Each day the water level was dropping and the guides were praying for rain. The first morning I fished a pool a mile below the camp. A fast broad stream. No fish showed but almost at once I missed a good rise, my fault being too quick on the strike. I was using my little single-handed greenheart, floating line and No. 6 fly. On the guide's advice I had put on a 20 lb leader. Next I got broken by something really big, and 30 lb fish were not unknown. Later I got a 6 lb grilse. The New Brunswick Government has, for conservation reasons, set a limit of two fish a day for each rod. In that first afternoon I got a salmon. This, with my grilse made up my quota for the day. So we motored back upstream to the camp. David came back also with the permitted limit, two salmon of 9 and 10 lbs. The camp like the others was a dry one, but this time David and I had taken the necessary precautions in our luggage. Then after that first day we could do nothing for three hot days. The water temperature rose to 72° and not a fish would move. On the fourth day came rain. By evening the water temperature was down to 61°. So fishing recommenced. "Steve", Air Vice Marshal Stevenson, an old friend of mine, and cousin of K.C. who lives in Vancouver, B.C., was looking after us wonderfully so even on the non-fishing days we never seemed to have a dull moment as we argued the problems of the world and cures for its ills. "Steve" came to the camp to stay with his cousin each year and he too had come fully armed in his luggage. When the rain came we had the permitted limit each day. One day David had two good fish by 10 a.m. So there was nothing for him to do all day but sit on the verandah or try for brown trout off the bank. With dry fly he got two or three of around ½ lb. We both tried the dry fly for salmon. We got a rise at nearly every cast but the fish never meant serious business. Our fly served merely to annoy them. They splashed beside the fly but had no intention of taking it. One morning we thought to try two pools upstream where the Kedgwick river ran into the Restigouche. We motored upstream for an hour and had a lot of fun, particularly when we discovered that the salmon showing in a deep very slack bit of water would take the fly. Our guides said, "No good trying these. They won't take in that slow stream." We found they did. In no time David and I were both broken by big fish. We picked out quite a few from this place. Great satisfaction to prove the experts wrong.

On the Sunday morning when we were due to fly back on the midnight Air Canada plane from Halifax, K.C. had his Jet Ranger land on a small cleared patch at the water's edge by the camp. We flew up the river past the old camp, not opened this year as there was the other one we were billeted in. Then we flew an aerial tour over some of the two million acres K.C. owns. We finished up landing at the Irving Airport where we left the helicopter and boarded a fast twin executive. In an hour and a half we landed at Halifax Airport. It was a hot Sunday afternoon and no one seemed interested in helping us unload luggage, nor were there any trucks which could take our kit and avoid quite a walk to the terminal building. Finally K.C. himself insisted on humping a big bag and between the pilot, David and myself, we made the Air Canada reservation desk. With grateful goodbyes, the executive left us to fly K.C. back to Saint John's. We had hours to kill, 5 p.m. to 11 p.m. and with no dollars to spare to rent a taxi into the city where Halifax on a Sunday afternoon is not exactly exciting and if we reached it there would have been nothing to do. Go to the "Inn on the Lake" we were told — only about seven miles off. This we did and found an excellent hotel-motel with a terrace where we could relax in the warm sun, sit, drink and enjoy looking across a small lake to the distant woods. We did a bit of equalising in alcohol for our week's great moderation and, to the surprise of the writer had a sequence of double "Old Fashioneds". Next we dined off fresh lobster with a bottle of white wine and about 10.10 p.m. we went to board our aircraft. I was lucky to be in the first class and just as David was passing me to go to the economy section in the rear, a steward said: "Here is your seat, Lord P.", waving him to a first class seat opposite mine. So David for that evening ceased to be an economy Mr P. and became a first class peer. We were shown a long and rich dinner menu with a fine choice of wines but all I wanted was a glass of water to take a sleeping pill and shut down for I was almost "out on my feet". Not so David. Two lovely girls, one a hostess and the other a captain's wife were the only other first class passengers. David was soon chatting them up and, to my intense admiration joined them in a comprehensive dinner sequence — cocktails, champagne, white wine, red wine and brandy. Full marks to youth for being capable of meeting this dinner challenge after our double old fashioneds before and hock at our motel dinner. I did have quite a job waking him up when we landed at Prestwick en route for Heathrow. But for my insistent shouting in his ear and shaking I believe he might have been left asleep, as immovable cabin residue after we landed at London Airport.

So ended for both of us a perfect 1976 fishing holiday.

CHAPTER EIGHT

The Maestro

THERE used to be an old song "Have you ever seen a dream walking?" My version is, "Have you ever seen Lee Wulffe fishing?" If, as is likely, you have not been as lucky as I have over this, then you have really missed something. Here is a man who, so the story goes, for a bet caught and landed a salmon on the fly without a rod. Here is a man who I have seen with my own eyes hook a 10 lb salmon on a little rod about 5′ long, light line and nylon leader, then turn his back to the river, put the rod over his shoulder and just walk the fish ashore.

Lee Wulffe is an international figure as a fisherman. His books and his fish photography have for years delighted we fishermen. All this was not enough for such a sportsman. He had to learn to fly his own little seaplane. All went well until one day, just before I first met him some twenty-five and more years ago, he had a little mishap landing in the sea. The seaplane turned turtle and Lee was rescued hanging on to one of the upturned floats but has continued to live to give the marine and fishing world volumes of the most beautiful coloured plates of many fish caught in waters all over the world.

Here I tell, as given to me, how Lee won his no-rod wager for a worth-while stake. With a party he was fishing a small, but rich in salmon, Newfoundland river when he accepted the bet. First, he put a reel with a floating line into his right hand jacket pocket. Next, he pulled off the length of line he thought would be needed to reach the fish when he waded out, allowing for a short leader on which he tied his fly. Correctly positioned in mid-stream, he allowed the measured length of line to float downstream of where he was standing in the water. Then he took the line between his thumb and index finger of his right hand and stretched out his arm at an angle of forty-five degrees above the horizontal. Lifting off the water

50

The Old Dee Bridge,

Braemar Castle

Loch Brora

A Morning on the Silly Little River — the author and George Murray

Speyside

Woodend, Deeside

Kelso Bridge, River Tweed

A Lucky Day at Tulchan: the author and Tom Purdey

The Dee

about half the total length of line he had taken from the reel, with a quick upward movement from the elbow joint of his forearm he whisked the fly off the water then allowed it to fall back and float. Next he let float down more line to the full length of his measure. Again the quick upward whisk. But this time from shoulder to elbow joined the forearm move so as to make one upward complete arm sweep. As the arm came down the line and fly flew forward. The fly touched the water; a salmon rose and took it. Lee's left hand dived into the right pocket to bring out the reel which he held firmly in an upright position while with his right hand he played the fish by hand-line until, quite quickly, he brought it to the net.

Some years ago there was much correspondence in *The Field* about why in Canada salmon can be caught on the dry-fly yet under similar weather conditions and water temperature in Scotland it just does not work. Eventually, at the instigation of several interested parties, Lee Wulffe was invited over as a guest on the Aberdeenshire Dee. The visit resulted in Lee giving demonstrations on how he fished dry-fly in Canada. Several times he rose salmon but failed to hook one. I remember the final summary in *The Field*: "Lee Wulffe has much to learn from the Dee — But the Dee has much to learn from Lee Wulffe."

My first meeting with Lee, now many years ago, was at Cornerbrook, Newfoundland, My wife and I had flown up at the kind invitation of the late Sir Eric Bowater, then Chairman of the Bowater Group of Companies. At that time, and for all I know now, you could say with truth that Cornerbrook town was Bowater for here was the great paper and pulp mill employing many hundreds on the job of turning timber logs into finished products, then to be carried in Bowater ships from Cornerbrook to different parts of the world. The extremely comfortable inn was Bowater owned. Shops and streets of houses belonged to Bowater. The hospital and local churches were mostly Bowater built and supported. The local head of this complex industrial empire was Monty Lewin, Bowater Director, ex-Naval officer and clearly a leader of men, ably helped and supported by his charming wife. When Monty heard from London of our forthcoming visit he laid on a three day fishing programme and managed to get Lee Wulffe as our expert help and guide. The plan was to fly in from Cornerbrook each morning to some different river. For this we were to use a twin-engined Grumman Amphibian which Bowater had chartered from the U.S.A. for the summer. The main job of the aircraft was to watch for forest fires and to photograph the Company's timber limits so as to build up a mosaic of the boundaries. The pilot was hired, also, with the charter. He had never before been north to Newfoundland. He was an early middle aged beaky-faced man who wore rimless pince-nez, always a still white collar and tie, a very shiny light blue suit and quite the most pointed toe black shoes I have ever seen. I do not know how much experience he had on Grummars but on one thing I was sure. To use a colloquialism, every time we took off he "scared the pants off me". The take-off run had to be in Cornerbrook harbour which held quite a few ships of different sizes from ocean-going to sailing dinghies. At the end of three days, entailing three harbour take-offs, some of them cross-wind, I felt there was not a ship's funnel I had not peered down nor a mast of a sailing ship that had not flashed past my window at almost touching distance nor various little rowing boats that had not just escaped death as they slipped under our wing just as we became airborne. Thank goodness it was under Lee Wulffe's guidance in the second pilot's seat on the flight-deck that we navigated over forest, lake and river most of which looked to me exactly the same in this undeveloped uninhabited distant land. The daily programme was for Monty and his wife to pick us up at the inn after breakfast in their car which had its boot filled with hampers of food and drink and all our fishing gear. Lee met us at the jetty where the Grummar lay alongside. Ourselves and supplies were loaded into the cabin as well as an inflatable rubber dinghy. The two Pratt and Whitney motors started up and from now on we were in pointed-toes' hands for better or worse, and we could do nothing about it. If I did not close my eyes on the take-off run I certainly held my breath. That first day we were to fly to a lake out of which the Serpentine River ran its short course of about twelve miles to the sea. This lake was in the centre of the Bowater timber reserve land. Now in Newfoundland all fishing being free subject to a Provincial Licence, in theory, therefore, the Serpentine was open to the public and any fisherman could enjoy its runs and pools all filled with salmon at the right season. But in practice the Serpentine was Bowater private preserve. From the sea the river was an impractical place to reach. You would need a power yacht or sailing ship with sleeping accommodation to work round the coast just to reach the river mouth. Having arrived, no canoe could ever have got up the rocky rapids and other hazards. From land, the lake on which we landed was not difficult to reach along several miles of side road off the main road. However, this would not get the would-be fisherman very far. Almost as soon as he turned off the main on to the side road he would face a heavily barred gate; several red warning notices and a guard house out of which would come a tough uniformed armed guard. This was one of the entrances to the Bowater timber reserve forests worth millions of dollars and which one careless lighted cigarette, or discarded match or undamped camp fire could set ablaze, and start one of the dreaded forest fires laying waste thousands and thousands of acres of valuable irreplaceable woodland. Since those days modern forest fire fighting equipment, use of water tank aircraft able to empty hundreds of tons on any fire, helicopters for transportation of fire fighting crews and equipment development have all helped to lessen the chances of catastrophe but great dangers still exist in dry summers. Small wonder that owners of vast timber reserves keep out all visitors who cannot produce an official permit. Every visitor like ourselves was asked to surrender matches and lighters. If the car had an electric cigarette lighter the driver was warned only to smoke within the car and take immense care to extinguish all cigarette ends or pipe ash. Thus the Serpentine River, free to all in theory, was in fact a private Bowater fishery.

From the Amphibian we canoed down river, landing at the head of a truly lovely looking pool, no wider than the Exe or Usk, which could be fished entirely from the bank. Fish were showing all over the pool. In no time we had grassed two on the bank. Then Lee Wulffe went into action. Using a small 5' split cane rod with a light reel to match, equally light line and leader, he waded out knee deep. In very few minutes he had hooked a good fish. He turned round back to the river, put the rod over his shoulder and casually walked ashore, talking to us all the time in a normal way. The fish just followed him and with a flap of its tail was on the shingle. Why the fish allowed itself to be pulled along without fight I just do not know. Lee said that he could almost always do this with a salmon in that sort of pool of swift but calm water. Our catch for the day was four salmon, the best 12 lb, a number of grilse, and sea trout running up to 4 lbs. We canoed to the Grummar, loaded the catch, took off and were back at Cornerbrook by tea time. Since our time Bowaters have built overlooking the best pool a highly attractive log-hutted camp for their visitors which, of course, means the Serpentine is no longer the almost unfished water of our expedition.

The next day we flew northwards from Cornerbrook landing on a lake just near where the "River of Ponds" River runs in. We seemed to be the sole inhabitants of what since then has become the location of one if not more popular fishing camps. Today one can from London book an air passage to Gander, air transport from Gander to the lake, be given a guide and canoe, be fed and generally cared for, all for a single inclusive fee. Alas; this fee is pretty stiff and, worse still, has to be paid in Canadian or U.S. dollars. To get ashore we lugged the inflatable dinghy through the cabin door and Lee paddled the party ashore in two loads. We built a depot and, with every care, got a camp fire going so as to cook freshly caught trout or salmon. Here, for the first time, I tried the dry-fly for salmon under instruction from Lee. We put on a big fuzzy floating fly and cast upstream at the point where the cold river water met the warmer lake. Wading was easy and safe. The salmon seemed highly excited as my fly drifted down over their heads. At every cast they rose beside the fly usually not touching it. Other times they knocked it or just rolled over it, pushing the fly under the water. Then very occasionally, one would take it. The fly would disappear under and here I learnt by the experience of several losses that one had to wait for the crucial second of the take and then strike quickly or the fish would spit out the fly. All that lovely hot afternoon I practiced on the many fish sufficiently interested to come up to the fly. By the end of the afternoon I had risen number beyond counting, pricked a lot of mouths and managed to land two. Never shall I forget those wonderful hours with the River of Ponds salmon attacking my dry fly.

On the way back, before taking off from the lake, Lee decided that we would taxi the Amphibian across and down some two miles to an inlet which he wanted to prospect for depth and obstructions with a view to a seaplane landing point not too far from another river he knew of and hoped to try. Once more we got out the rubber dinghy, inflated it and paddled ashore. To my surprise from out of the woods came a figure in ragged woodman's clothes, unkempt, long grey hair, unshaven cheeks, but a lovely pair of clear blue eyes. He greeted Lee cheerfully for as a Forest Ranger he had met him before. Seeing that we were obvious "city folk" he asked where we came from. I told him England and then he said something I have always remembered. It brought tears to my eyes. This grand old-timer asked, "And how's the old country doing?". He had never been to England. He had been born and brought up in Newfoundland. His father had come as a Scottish emigrant many years before. But to him, England was still the loved "old country". I hope the choke in my throat may be understood and forgiven.

Our third day's expedition had to be washed out because of bad flying weather. In two days I had learnt much, enjoyed such fishing as hitherto had been a dream and in company of such kind and generous friends. I judged myself then, as now, a lucky man.

CHAPTER NINE

A Minnow into Poland

STRAIGHT away let me make clear this chapter has less to do with fishing than International Politics. Yet it was just one cast of mine that caused telegraph wires to hum, inter-Governmental protests to be drafted, sentries to level rifles and a harrassed British Government representative to be called in to prevent my probable arrest.

It all happened a good many years ago when the map of Europe showed three small brave independent Baltic states, Lithuania, Latvia and Estonia created from Germany's defeat after the First World War. The people of these three states now enjoyed freedom from German domination; something approaching democratic government and great national pride. Today as a result of Soviet expansion they have disappeared and their peoples crushed into the maw of Russian Communism.

There was a Member of Parliament, Sir Alfred Bossom, M.P. for Maidstone, who took these little Baltic states under his wing. He fought ceaselessly between the two wars, in and out of Parliament, on behalf of their political and economic interests. The three Governments recognised to the full Sir Alfred's work on their behalf and rewarded him with suitable honours. In full dress and white tie Sir Alfred was indeed a fine sight. Silver stars glittered on the lapels of his tail coat, ribbons round the collar, a line of miniatures all of high Baltic Orders made Sir Alfred on any formal occasion outshine everyone, even the highest in the land. Lord Mountbatten with full medals would look almost naked compared to Sir Alfred.

It was way back in 1934 that Sir Alfred invited three other M.P.'s to accompany him on an unofficial Parliamentary Delegation as guests of the Governments of Lithuania, Latvia and Estonia. He did me the honour of an invitation which I accepted with alacrity. Being a keen fisherman, I thought, "Here is an exciting chance of trying new waters". My enquiries at the respective three Embassies in London produced little result. No one seemed to have heard of fishing for fun. Wires flew back and forth between embassies and governments with final news that in Lithuania, down near the Polish border there was "fine fishing". For what sort of fish I could not find out. I decided to go out to Lithuania a few days before the rest of the delegation were due, and in my luggage I included flies, trout reels, spinning baits and all the rest. For rods I decided on a 3-piece single handed stiff 9 ft trout rod and a light spinning rod. In due course, via Berlin, I reached Kovno, capital of Lithuania. The city contained one small but clean hotel; some few shops and in the streets quietly dressed happy-looking citizens with healthy red-cheeked children, a fine State Opera House, one cinema and lots and lots of Government Offices and Military Barracks. That was Kovno — that was — in the early thirties. By the end of day one I had made contact with Mr Preston, our British representative, met various officials, been invited to dine that evening with the Army Chief of Staff. I felt with all these kind hospitable official folk I must be well on the way to the river of "fine fishing" which everyone I met had never been near. I wanted to be off the next day but in twenty-four hours this strange Englishman had been drawn into the narrow social life of Kovno high society. That night at dinner I broached the subject of the river but was told before I thought of fishing I just had to join in the Government wild boar shoot organised for the next day. After breakfast next morning I found myself in an open Mercedes sitting between the Minister of Transport and a beautiful lady who I was told was his mistress but also the leading lady at that evening's performance at the State Opera, to which I was expected and for which a place had been reserved for me in the Ministerial box. Beside the driver sat a fully armed soldier. After an hour's drive through flat wooded country interspersed by small-holding farms with poor buildings, we turned off the main road to rendezvous in a grass carpeted clearance in the middle of a pine forest. Already half a dozen official cars were there and though only 10 a.m. their passengers were seated on rugs in a semi-circle well advanced in liquid consumption. Each passenger had brought with him a hamper of sandwiches, cakes, and most important of all, sets of little silver cups with accompanying bottles. With much bowing I was introduced to each of the circle; the Prime

Minister, Deputy Prime Minister, Minister of Police, General of the Army and a whole series of officials. As I shook hands with each I was handed one of the little silver cups filled with vodka or some fiery local spirit distilled, I believe, from apple juice. My hosts each drank my health "no heel taps" and I was expected to reciprocate in turn. There was still no sign of the shoot but the party went on with increasing fervour. Very soon the exchanging of cups became like quick passing of the sixpence in "Up Jenkins". Two things became quite clear to me. First, that my arrival was giving a splendid opportunity for a grand drinking party "on the Government". Secondly that if there was to be any shooting I wanted to be as far away from it as I could. An officer girt with sword and in full dress walked up, saluted and announced the beaters, troops brought out by lorry from Kovno barracks, were ready and lined up at the edge of the forest some half mile away. The Prime Minister managed, with some difficulty, to rise to make a little speech, including a welcome to myself and to announce the shoot would now commence. At this point we lost one senior Ministerial colleague who just lay down and passed out, although no one seemed to take any notice. From some motor vehicle a whole armoury of weapons was produced. I was handed a double barrelled 8-bore shot gun, so weighty that I could scarcely have got it to my shoulder, which fortunately I never had to. I was given four cartridges and through the celluloid ends I saw in each two large torpedo-shaped lead shots. What powder load, or weight, or killing power these cartridges had I did not know. Of one thing I was quite determined, I was not going to find out by firing that gun.

The green velvet suited game warden advised through an interpreter that the centre of the fifteen guns was the most likely spot to get a shot. There was some argument when I insisted on the flank position but I won, and was escorted by an officer in full dress to the far edge of the forest. There I stood for perhaps an hour and a half and, thank heavens, saw nothing and heard only one shot somewhere far down the line. Then the beaters appeared through the trees: "Shoot over" I was told. No one had seen a wild boar. The single shot was at a rabbit and a miss at that. Back to the cars and celebration drinks to mark the end of the sport followed by a fine road race of Government cars back to Kovno where I had hoped to relax. Alas: no sleep for the weary for at 5 p.m. I was due at the one tea shop where the smart set of Kovno met every afternoon for the "cinq heure". Hot chocolate and whipped cream was the standard fare and here I met the fascinating, brave, beautiful, impoverished, tragic, but still irrepressible, Russian family of Sheremetensky, the "haute monde" of Kovno. There was Prince and Princess Sheremetensky, and the young Princess Tatiana, a lovely girl of twenty who spoke five languages, and the seventeen-year-old Princess Olga Sheremetensky. The Prince had been a member of the Russian Duma, and was considered politically a very Liberal left wing man. Alas, now they had become refugees from Russia with lands and property confiscated. At Kovno they waited in optimistic expectation that each day the one daily post would bring official news of their long promised compensation for sequestrated forests. Directly this arrived, as it surely must, the Prince and Princess with the Princesses Tatiana and Olga would take that night's train to Berlin to start there a new life. At tea time each day, long farewells were touchingly made for tomorrow surely the compensation money would have arrived and the family would be happily on their way. Alas, this never seemed to come about and each week Kovno society noted sadly that the beautiful pearl necklace of the Princess Sheremetensky had one less pearl. Soon these afternoon farewells became a Kovno jest entered into by all, including the Prince and Princess. At the break up of the 5 p.m. the tender goodbyes were followed by: "Dear Princess we will see you all tomorrow at the same time". I never heard in after years how Prince and Princess Sheremetensky and the lovely Princesses Tatiana and Olga fared. I guess so long as men are men these Princesses were all right.

At the State Opera than night I really got down to plans for my trip to the "fine fishing" river. The Minister of Transport promised me a car and driver who could speak a little English for early next day. Armed with rods, reels, tackle, food and the inevitable bottle of schnapps I was away from my hotel by 8 a.m. A two hour drive and we came to the river running alongside the main road. To meet us was the local gendarme. The "fine fishing river" about 30 yards wide looked good: clean fast water, rocks and eddies but what it held in the way of fish I had to find out for myself. I was on the Lithuanian bank and opposite the bank was Polish territory for this was a boundary river between two not very friendly countries.

I thought the best chance of finding out what the river held was to try a small Devon minnow. I started with a short cast at the head of a run. I fished down lengthening my cast until the bait was landing well over the other side. Suddenly I had a fierce under-water take but before I could give attention to the fish, whatever it was, I heard a shout from the opposite bank and found myself looking down the barrel of a gun aimed at me by a uniformed soldier. I could not understand one word of what he was calling out but his meaning was all too clear. He did not at all approve of my fishing and made signs that I must pull in my line. That fish, and what that fish was, I shall never know — my guess is a pike — was off the hook when I started to reel in. I stood on the bank wondering why all this was happening. My gendarme came up beside me doing his share of shouting and gesticulating at the soldier on the opposite bank who by now had stopped pointing his rifle at my head. However, the rifle soon came back into action again, this time not at me but at the gendarme for he too had drawn a large pistol from his belt, which he proceeded to point across the river at the soldier. The shouting was intense but what each could hear across the river I could not tell. What I do know is the gun pointing went on, each waiting for the other to fire the first shot. With as much dignity as I could muster I retreated back to the car. My gendarme lowered his pistol. The soldier lowered his rifle. My gendarme came to the car. The soldier disappeared into the forest.

All this excitement and two things were clear to me. First that with one cast my dreams of the river of "fine fishing" were finished with; secondly that according to the broken English of my driver, the soldier on the opposite bank was a Polish border guard who saw my minnow land well over the middle line of the river and thus I had violated Polish territory.

When I got back to Kovno I found waiting for me in the hotel front hall three solemn-faced men: a worried looking Mr Preston, and two officials. Mr Preston explained the one in the plain clothes was a senior member of the Foreign Office and the other, in uniform, the Commandant of the Border Guards. Already the wires between Cracow and Kovno had been buzzing. The Polish Government had telegraphed top priority that someone, presumably a spy, had appeared on the river bank on the Lithuanian side and started fishing in Polish waters. This, the Polish Government said, was a serious affair;

in any event a blatant affront to Poland and quite possibly a case of espionage. Explanations were demanded of Lithuania together with assurance that the matter would at once be investigated and the culprit arrested and punished. The Lithuanian officials had been sent to investigate. Hearing tell of the English M.P. visitor they contacted Mr Preston. Their orders were to report back urgently to the Prime Minister for just then relations were delicate and Lithuania had a particular wish not to offend Poland. I went over the story of how I had made just one cast: that if my minnow had gone over the "via Medium", as it had, I was quite innocent of any sinister purpose: that in Britain, provided one fished from on one's own bank or if wading not over the half way across, one could cast over into the further water. Anyhow the Lithuanian Government officials seemed to accept and understand my story and I was assured that all this would be explained that evening to the Polish Government. This business dealt with, the four of us got down to some steady fire water drinking which I provided gladly and thankfully.

After that day I gave up all ideas of trying the river of "fine fishing", went upstairs to pack tackle and put the rods away.

Thus I was able to meet my fellow M.P.'s next day a free man and not prisoner in a Lithuanian prison cell. And so ended the International Incident of a Minnow into Poland.

CHAPTER TEN

Norway

HER name was *Venus* and she was a Victorian. Her age betrayed her. She lay alongside the Newcastle quay while well-scented black smoke seeped from her one funnel. It was mid-afternoon in the summer of 1923 and at 6 p.m. she was due to sail for Stavanger carrying a handful of passengers, including our family party bound for a fishing holiday in Norway. Lying just beyond her was one of the two smart looking twin screw turbine ships, *Leda* and *Jupiter*, which did the swift comfortable twice-weekly run to Bergen. *Venus* was far from smart. Her lines betrayed her age. Her engines, working a single screw, were old-fashioned reciprocating. When you walked along the companion-way to the passenger accommodation aft you passed an open well exposing pistons working to and fro and great cranks throwing themselves in circles just missing your head. At the end of the companion-way you came to the saloon shaped to a curving taper that finished with the rudder post casing. In the centre of the saloon was the one dining table for all the passengers. Places were already laid for the evening meal and exposed to eye and nose was a formidable collection of Norwegian cheeses of every shape and smell. There was no ventilation below deck so already lying in harbour the air reeked of hot oil, fish and cheese. Off the saloon were doors opening into the few double bunk cabins. I knew three things. First: that this was to be our home for the next two to three days, the voyage time depending on weather. Secondly: that being right in the stern we were to have the unique chance of being lifted high up and then crashed down as soon as we met any sea. Of course this up and down see-saw could be varied by sideways barrel rolls as soon as the sea was on one quarter. Thirdly: that the Captain was looking forward to a rough North Sea passage.

As we dropped down the Tyne a loud gong announced dinner was ready. We bowed politely to the three men passengers who emerged from their cabins. I gathered later that these were three Norwegian business men who had come over to discuss matters concerning the export of Norwegian fish, fresh, salted and tinned. Only one could speak a little English. What happened to the three I never discovered. Whether they shut themselves up in their cabins or went off to the ship's company mess I do not know for we never saw them again until we docked in Stavanger harbour. The meal started with thick pea soup and this went down all right even though with the last spoonfuls we sensed the first pitch. After the soup came a greasy meat stew, but by then the ship's motion had become violent. The table rose and fell as we hit the open sea. Just under the saloon floor was the propeller shaft. At all times under steam it gave a steady groaning noise but now, as the stern lifted up and down, the poor thing gave off terrific vibrations at the propeller's effort first to claw through waves then, as if lifted clear and starved of sea water, it did a little mid-air race, before plunging once again into the next wave. This was all too much for our party, including myself. One by one we got up in silence from the table and disappeared into the cabins. I took a last farewell look at the cheeses and, admitting prospective defeat, retired to my bunk. Lying down I felt fairly safe. I closed my eyes, tried to think ahead of a lovely river full of fish and dozed off. Throughout the long night's intermittent sleep I woke periodically as after a high lift up there was a terrific crash as the stern fell into the trough of a wave. From groans and shakings I knew that poor old single screw was having the hell of a night too. I shut down in my cabin until the morning of the third day when I felt the ship's motion was no more. I looked out of my porthole to see we were just docking. All the corpses had revived and we met on deck, pale, but determined. That afternoon we travelled in a little local steamer, through the fiord to our destination, the little village of Aardal. Our first sight of the house rented with the Aardal river was depressing. No lovely little fishing-lodge but a villa on the outskirts of a fishing hamlet. The country around was flat and the surroundings of small farms dreary. By later afternoon the rain had started and altogether the arrival did not bode well; things got no better the more we investigated and the longer we stayed. Our fisherman, engaged with the let, said there were practically no salmon in the river. Most of them had already gone up several miles over the falls to water which was not our fishing. He expected no further run of fish that season. Maybe, he said, we shall get some sea trout. I forget now how many salmon were caught during our two weeks but I know the total could be counted on one hand. I caught none for I was highly inexperienced. The brightest time for me was when the little river, for very small it was, came down in flood. I had a 6 ft spinning rod and an Ariel reel. I went down to the bridge and saw more small fish moving and showing than I had ever dreamt of. I knew just enough to realise I had arrived as a sea trout run was on. With every cast of my spinner I hooked a fish. Most were herling (small sea trout) with an occasional fish of 2 lbs. I think by the time I had finished and the run past I must have caught enough to feed half the village. The Aardal expedition was really a flop. The agent through whom the let had been made had certainly taken us for a real ride. There was nothing to be done about it and when the two weeks was up and once again we boarded the *Venus*, bound for Newcastle, I don't think any of us were sad.

The year following the same family party went to the Stjordaal river north of Trondheim. Here the house was comfortable; the river fair and we managed to catch a few salmon of no great distinction in size or number.

It was not until my third summer visit that I began to understand and enjoy Norway. That year we made the first of three successive August fishings of the Eire River, famed for its big fish. To get to the Eire you first had to cross from Newcastle to Bergen and this time we left Newcastle quay in the comfortable large Fred Olsen line twin screw *Jupiter*. As we steamed out into the mid-stream there alongside and just below where the *Jupiter* had been moored was the same old *Venus* of four years before still with the same plume of strong smelling smoke belching forth from her one funnel. I raised my hat to her and went below to the bar. From Bergen we took passage overnight in a coastal steamer to Molde. Poor Molde was knocked about in the last war. Shelled, bombed and occupied by German forces its citizens had suffered grievously physically and materially. But when we landed on that sunny peaceful afternoon of the late twenties all that pain, anguish and destruction lay in the future. We bundled into a hire car and started our forty mile drive to the Eire. For much of the journey we clung to the coast with calm deep looking dark water on our right flank. To the left there were wooded sloping hills leading up to towering rocky mountains. We twisted and turned on the winding road until quite suddenly after about an hour and a half we came round a corner and there in front of us the hills separated to leave between them a green valley of fields with grazing cattle, neat farm houses and barns intersected by a glittering stream of water. We were looking straight up the valley of the Eire. That glittering stream was the lower reach of the river. Far up the valley, maybe five miles, we could see a cascade of white water making the falls above which salmon could not pass until enough rain gave opportunity for their strength to battle against torrent and current in their urge to obey the command of nature to spawn in the upper lake and in the little mountain streams.

At the mouth where the river ran into the fiord the Eire was around a hundred yards wide. Ascend a quarter of a mile and it had become a medium sized stream something around the average width of the middle stretches of the Aberdeenshire Dee. The current was swift only slowing appreciably when the river opened up into one of its several pools the size of a big pond. There were no banks as such. Only vertical rock face leading up to mountain pinnacles which looked to anyone in a boat below to be pointing straight up to heaven. It was in these circular shaped pools where the water was deep and the current slowed that the big fish lurked. The only way to fish them was to "harle". In case some reader is a stranger to harling I will endeavour to explain. First, harling is undoubtedly the dullest, most boring form of salmon fishing. Your boatman pulls the boat to the head of the pool and into one bank. You have with you two — not one — salmon rods. With a rod in each corner of the stern he pulls out and at once the current catches hold. It is here where the skill and strength of the boatman come right into the picture. He holds the boat steady on the edge of the current while with first one and then the other rod you slowly pay out maybe twenty yards of line. At once, as the current takes hold and your boatman defies its efforts to take you downstream the tip of the spinning rods begin to quiver with the vibrations of the wobbling spoons. You then adjust the pay out so as to give two different lengths of line for the two spoons. The longer one, thirty yards behind the boat, works deeper in the water than the other spoon with only twenty yards of line out. In this way you hope to cover fish lying at different depths. Losing no distance downstream the boatman rows head on to the current right across to the other bank. Arrived there, he lets the boat down two or three yards then starts across the river again. The fast stream all the time keeps the spoon bait wobbling, or spinning if it is a minnow. In due course at some point in the criss-cross search of the pool a fish takes hold of one of the baits offered. The boatman's job is then to grab the rod which has not been struck and reel the line in so that one does not foul the other. From this outline description of harling it can be appreciated how it is the dullest form ever of salmon fishing. There is no skill needed either for casting a fly or a spinning bait. There is no need to have the experience of looking at a pool and knowing by instinct the likely lies of the fish you are after. In harling the fish just hooks itself and provided the holder of the rod keeps it upright, lets the fish run and avoids a sort of tug of war, reels in whenever the fish allows, then finally the fish will be either netted or gaffed.

On the Eire most of our fish were caught harling or casting out a juicy red prawn with enough lead to be sure the prawn got right down to fish lying near the bottom. All too few fish were caught on the fly: only an occasional one.

The river ran about two hundred yards from our fishing lodge. Over the river at the nearest point to the lodge there was a footbridge crossing. The most exciting moment of the day was after breakfast when the whole party marched down to the bridge to peer into the deep clear water. Straight below and a few yards down there were some big rocks which made a sure and restful lie for fish straight in from the sea. Each morning we looked into the clear stream to count that day's new arrivals. These fish, fresh from the sea, were usually good "takers". It was the privilege of whoever's turn it was to fish the lower water to have first go at these fresh fish. The bridge must have been fifteen feet high above the water, and the water some eight feet deep. The method was to hold the rod straight downwards with a good weight fixed on the line some five feet above the bait. First we would try a spoon. In the fast current, the spoon surface flashed in the sunlight as it wobbled. Careful letting out and pulling in line could bring the spoon right across the fish's nose. Most often the fish would take no notice beyond swishing its tail and sometimes moving out of the way of this unwanted shining disturber of its rest.

Occasionally; very occasionally, the fish would make a grab and be hooked but this we found was extremely rare so the next stage was put into operation. The spoon was taken off the cast and a beautiful luscious red prawn was bound by wire to the needle which went through its body and which had two hooks attached. When properly mounted the hooks were hidden by being bound close to the underside of the prawn. The same lead weight as for the spoon and then the prawn was lowered until it moved gently in the deep water current back and forth in front of the nose of the salmon. One of two things happened. Either the fish at the sight and the smell of the prawn would rush away to get clear of this intrusion or he would show interest by an increased tail movement. This was the moment for steady nerves. Prepare for action. Sometimes the salmon might make one sudden violent rush and take the prawn in his mouth or he might swim round it, sniffing, snout hitting, but declining to do anything more serious or exciting. This indecision and playing about might go on for minutes followed by a furious grab. Whichever way the attack was made as soon as one saw the prawn taken and felt the line tighten you should strike and strike hard. The next urgent and vital task was to get to the end of the bridge and climb down on to the river bank, still with rod upright and line taut but trying not to tease or annoy unduly the hooked fish until you were safely treading green grass. After that the contest was really on. Sometimes the salmon won by spitting out prawn and hooks. Sometimes even though well hooked, the tackle would fail from the strain through broken hook or broken gut. More often, I like to think, the battle was won for the fisherman and lost for the fish. I reckon a rough guide for the time of contest is one minute for every pound weight. One day I had a fresh run thirty-five pounder from the bridge and I reckon he took the full thirty-five minutes to get him on to the bank.

With the post-breakfast bridge session over, the party would separate over five miles or so of water to meet again for lunch in the lodge. Very different from Aardal, the Eire Lodge was comfortable. The two Norwegian staff that went with the let were buxom, cheerful and to them, no work, even to washing all our clothes, was too much trouble. The lodge and its small garden were bounded by rich pasture meadows. On three sides rocky mountains towered. On the fourth we looked straight down the sea-water fiord. Strawberries and raspberries we had every day. As the crop at valley level became exhausted more would arrive each day from high, then higher ground. It was August: hot sun, blue skies and a seemingly never ending supply of fresh fruit. Our final fruit-consignment came from a farm way up in the hills. After lunch there was sleep. Then about 6 p.m. out again until eleven or later for it never became really dark and you can read a newspaper at midnight.

I forget how many fish we caught in three weeks. Not many, but their size was enormous. Not all the party were experienced fishermen. We had one, to me in those days, elderly member; a Colonel Chevenix-Trench. He had never caught a salmon but longed to do so. And he did: the two biggest weighing 54 and 57 lbs. We put the Colonel in charge of Conrad, senior boatman, six feet four inches tall, grizzled hair and moustache who had given a lifetime's service to the love of his life, the Eire river. Conrad took the Colonel to one of the pond size deep smooth pools. He instructed the Colonel how to let out line, put full check on reels and put the rods one out at an angle at each corner of the stern. He told him what to do if a fish struck. He was to pick up the rod, hold it vertical and not pull against the fish but let it run if it so wished. Meanwhile, Conrad would be reeling in the other rod, thus avoiding danger of a confused muddle of the lines with the almost inevitable loss of the fish. A fish did strike. The Colonel forgot his orders. He kept the rod with its point almost in the water. He started to hold the line and commenced a tug-of-war contest which the fish must surely win. Conrad bawled at the Colonel with the little bit of English he knew: "No, No," he shouted. "Feesh big one. Bigger than you. No lose or I kill you." Poor Colonel, flustered and fearful just put the rod down on the boat's seat, turned to Conrad and said: "All right — just kill me. It's better that way than not knowing what to do." Finally some sort of accommodation on what to do was arrived at even though the Colonel obstinately held the rod horizontal to the water. After about 50 minutes of error corrected by Conrad shouting, Conrad gaffed from the shore a giant of 59 lbs. Conrad's remark deserves to be recorded by all fishermen. "Everything wrong but fish in boat!" Later and with less anguish the Colonel was again runner-up in the weight contest with a 54 pounder. This time he kept both his head and the rod upright. For myself, I got a 47 pounder, also harling. Frankly it did not give much fun. It just pulled and pulled: it fought deep and slow. The tackle was strong and the fish well hooked and it was like nothing so much as having a man on the end of your line. Give me every time a fresh run spring fish of twelve pounds caught on light tackle, small fly and floating line. This Norway harling in the Eire certainly yielded great fish but to me it is not the weight that counts but the fun of hooking, playing and landing all on your own. For this give me Scotland or Canada, grateful as I always shall be for the chance of fishing in Norway for these great fish.

CHAPTER ELEVEN

The Chapter of Shame

THIS is my confession. I know that deep down I have the instincts of a poacher. Why I have not had to give play to this sinful inclination (at least not much and not very often) is because I have been lucky in my fishing and have had no need. Let me make clear at once that I draw a distinction between poaching and the poacher. Poaching can mean dastardly criminal acts, the legal penalties for which are far too light. Cymag or other poison, netting, spearing, snatching: all of these and some other wholly nefarious practices I abhor in common with all decent people, fishermen or otherwise. Now to me the poacher, a lone man who casts his fly, or worm, where he should not in the hopes of getting "one for the pot" with no thought of commercial profit is in a different class to gang poaching. Of course, he must be apprehended; turned off the water and warned severely against repetition of his misdemeanor. We just cannot have stray anglers covering the water which is carefully preserved and costly to maintain. But to me he is a wrongdoer for whom I have a feeling of understanding even as he is turned off. I am lucky to be on the water by every right. He, too, is a sportsman who is trying his skills in a proper manner, though doing this when and where he has no right. On salmon water he just must be told to clear off, but in doing this you can talk to him reasonably. Certainly in Scotland, if he is a stranger, you can advise him about local Angling Associations which usually have day tickets for visitors and can often be rewarding for the real tryer. Salmon fishing in Scotland need not be the rich man's preserve, as sometimes politicians like to declare in the House of Commons. Years ago we stayed at Garve and I went to the local Angling Association in Strathpeffer and paid £1 a day for a rod on a stretch of the Common. It was mid-week and I had the water to myself. Of course, when the water level shot up and down without notice due to operation of the Hydro-Electric, fishing was hopeless.

Nevertheless for my £1 a day for 3 days I had a fish a day. For some years I owned the Ardmiddle beat on the Deveron. Two beats below me there was a long stretch of water which the Forglen estate gives over to the Turiff Angling Association which, in turn, issues visitors' permits. On the Deveron relations between the Association and riparian owners were of the very friendliest, as I am sure is the case today. Each season each riparian owner invited the local Association as guests for the day on their stretch. No holds were barred either as regards flies, lures or baits or the number of rods fishing, and it was all great fun. The River Spey carries several good stretches as do many other rivers let to local Angling Associations who issue day tickets.

On the Brora, the local Association lets boats and day tickets for salmon, sea trout and brown trout on Loch Brora obtained through that splendid sportsman, Rob Wilson, in his tackle shop. There is also a stretch of the Lower Brora reserved for the Association.

Finally, I cannot leave out what I know of my own locality in Sutherland. Our little spate river, the Fleet, where you have literally to be on the water at the right hour when she rises, has some of the best pools given over by the three proprietors in the Strath, being Canbusmore, Morvich and Rovie. Alas, on our Tressady bit it is too small and too short carrying really only one rod, and certainly not more than two. However, Tressady tried to do its sharing by handing over Loch Muie to the Rogart Angling Association plus two Saturday rods on another Loch. So when I find the real fisherman gone wrong, while I do my duty, I try to suggest to him where he can go rightfully and enjoy what we are lucky enough to possess. I am quite sure local Angling Associations are the best guardians against local poaching. In the early '50's we owned Upper Hendersyde. There we let our trout fishing for 1/-d a year (which was not paid) to the Kelso Angling Association. They watched the river carefully and there was no poaching there. Twice I can remember a trout angler catching a salmon, and according to the rules, the angler who caught it had to report with the fish to the riparian owner. In both these cases, this was done and I asked how and where the fish had been caught. I thanked the man for bringing it to me, wished him good luck and had the pleasure of telling him to take the fish back to his home. I am convinced that owners can only continue to own fishings so long as we try to share with others in a reasonable way. Local Angling Associations understand the very real economic problems of ownership far better than Whitehall or St Andrew's House, and they appreciate first-hand the real problems of conservation. They realise that it is just political nonsense talked about opening all fishings to everyone and that very soon there would be nothing to open up except empty rivers. The trout fisherman in Scotland fishing without permission is quite a problem for Scottish laws are complex and understood by few. The only way to keep a persistent poacher off the water is by interdict from the Court. However, in practice, the unauthorised fisherman, technically a poacher even if fishing fly, usually clears off when he is warned. One day I found a man fishing for trout on our Fleet. I had the usual tale that "someone" had told him that it was all right to fish where he was. I found he was a man from Glasgow on holiday, an engineer. He had come a long way and after I had explained to him that he shouldn't be there, I hadn't the heart to spoil his day. I told him to carry on and enjoy himself and I could not have received a kinder letter than the one from him which the postman delivered the next day. I believe we ought to treat every case of unauthorised fishing on the merits and circumstances of that particular instance.

I return to my basic weakness; the instincts of a poacher. Have I ever poached or been a party to poaching? How many fisherman can put their hands on their hearts and say they are innocent. I cannot, but feel certain I am in good company.

In the early twenties I had my first experience of salmon fishing. My then father-in-law, Sir Robert Harvey, used to take the Fochabers beat on the Spey every February. The beat started above Fochabers Bridge, and I still remember the pools, Chapel, Dipple, Cruive Dyke. In those days it was strictly fly only. We fished with 16 or 17 ft greenheart rods, sunk line and a great heavy Alexander fly. Fish were plentiful and I caught my first salmon early in February in Dipple. Fly only was the strict order on the river. Now, somewhere in the picture of my memory comes a famous fisherman character of those days, Major McCorquadale. Either he fished somewhere up river or he may have owned the top water above our beat. Anyhow, his reputation was that of a great and severe laird. He always liked to catch more fish than anyone else and if his was not top score of the day the Major was irate. However, he always seemed to manage to be number one on the list. The story went that he was walking along the river bank with his ghillie and another fisherman. For some reason he was carrying his own fishing bag. The Major tripped and fell. Out of the bag his tackle came to rest in the heather. Unfortunately, one of the tackle boxes fell open. Out of it spilled a whole lot of lovely big red prawns! Within hours the secret of the Major's success was passed up and down the Spey. Such was his ferocity and his tenants' fears of being crossed off the rental list that no one dared speak of this terrible exposure except with baited breath and in a whisper.

Confession, they say, is good for the soul, so here goes.

About 1946 I took from the Department of Agriculture in Scotland the fishing of the Staffyn river in Skye, a pretty little stream which runs through heather country and holds salmon and sea trout but only after a spate. I had been warned that it was heavily poached directly there was enough rain to raise the water level to let the fish in from the sea. As soon as I arrived I got my intelligence service going and soon found out who was the leading local poacher. He was a fine young man and in no time I had taken him on as my ghillie and guardian of the river. The river level was dead low. The sun shone brightly each day; no fish were coming in and after two futile days flogging little pools without the sight of a fish, I told Jock that I was pretty fed up with it. By that time we were good friends and he said to me: "Would you like to feel your rod bend? Would you like a fish?" I said, "Yes." "All right," he said, "I'll show you how to get one."

We went up on the moor to a deserted pool of calm water perhaps three feet deep. There were rocks showing all up and down the pool. Jock took off his cap and placed it on the end of his long shepherd's crook. Carefully, slowly, gently he worked his way towards a showing rock. He crouched behind it and with one arm extended over the water held his stick with his hat on the end. This took all the glare off the surface of the water and allowed his keen eyes to scan the bottom of the river all round the rock. He nodded to me and withdrew from the bank with the same caution he showed to get out to the rock. "There's a fish lying under the rock," he said, "with its tail just showing." He made me go further down the river where I could cross to the other bank. When I arrived opposite the rock he was in position again. I had to cast my fly across the river to him. He took it into his hand and then very, very gently lowered his right arm into the water. Another nod to say he was going into action. As quick as lightning an upward move and the fly was into the fish somewhere just above the tail. The rod bent, the reel screamed, as the foul-hooked 7 pounder rushed downstream. After a lot of fun we beached him safely. Was it wicked? Yes. I suppose so but it was great sport and the only possible way to get a fish out of that river under the conditions prevailing.

In due course we had rain. I fished normally and got salmon and sea trout. Then the river went down again but in doing so it left a rush bordered sheet of water alongside the sea pool about 70 yards long and 20 wide. Between this pool of water and the main river there was no communication. But trapped in the pool was one salmon. We saw the water furrows as the fish shot up the pool when we walked by. Jock was determined we should have that fish. I had never seen before or since a salmon hunted by dogs, but Jock ordered his sheep dog to work the pool from one end to the other, backwards and forwards, through the reeds and across the water. Sure enough the dog did his job thoroughly. There was a swirl and a wave the length of the pool as the dog "put up" the salmon. The poor fish thought he was safe taking refuge under a rock at one end of the pool. But he had reckoned without Jock who had that fish out within minutes. Were we wicked? Yes, I suppose so, but it was terrific fun and I had learnt a lot and seen something I had never expected to have a chance of seeing — salmon hunted by dogs.

What bait or lure is allowed varies river by river. In Sutherland nearly everywhere it is fly only. On the Tweed the prawn is a recognised permissible bait and the late Duke of Roxburghe used to reserve for himself the first prawning day on Lower Floors. I confess that at times I have itched to dive into my bag and put up a prawn on some river where prawn is frowned on, if not actually forbidden. The fish are there and they just won't look at anything, fly or minnow. Prawn is the only hope. Have I ever done this? Certainly not on a river where I had been a guest, but on some high-priced rented stretch where the "stretch" has also been applied to the recorded bags submitted by the selling agents. Have I? I give no answer. Prawn on a light rod with no weight beyond one lead shot, cast up stream can be truly exciting. Sometimes the fish just rushes to seize the prawn; sometimes you just feel it nibbling and playing around for five to ten minutes before it decides to "have a go". I have fished in Norway, and here again the prawn is a recognised bait. I have always flogged the fly until I know it is hopeless, then, why not try the prawn? One thing I have learnt. If in the first few casts over fish they won't look at a prawn chuck it . . . Never flog the prawn like the fly.

Now the worm. Go on the little Sutherland Borgie river where fishermen naturally and always carry a tin of worms. No spinning allowed, but worm. Yes. And again, why not if the fly conditions are hopeless. "Have you any worms to spare," is almost a usual greeting on the Borgie from one fisherman to another. It's not poaching here and why should it be in lots of other rivers, particularly in flood, with water badly discoloured.

I leave this "Chapter of Shame" to be judged guilty or acquitted by my companion fishermen.

CHAPTER TWELVE

Would You Like To Own A Fishing?

HERE is a question, maybe a silly one, that many salmon fishermen must have asked themselves. Silly because before it can be answered you would have to know details of the choice offered you. Even so, I ask it in general terms just as I give reply in general terms.

Would you prefer to own some rather indifferent water on a rather second class river where in a good year you might get, say, thirty salmon or would you prefer renting a rod for two weeks of the best month each year on a first class river where, in good conditions, you ought to get two or three fish each day. For myself there is no doubt of my choice. I would go for my own little piece of water. Once having owned a fishing you know a satisfaction that even renting the famous Delfur beat on the Spey cannot give. On your own bit of river you may have just two pools and one run. There may be weeks when you know there is not a fish in the water but the day comes when someone, the gardener, the postman or a friend says, "I saw a fish in your water today". The challenge is on. You seize your rod and off you go to explore. The chances are that you will see nothing but that does not matter. There is a fish somewhere in your pool and somehow have him you will. Quite likely you will never see or touch him with fly or bait before the next rise of water comes when he will, for sure, move on upstream. Even so, the mere knowledge of that fish has given you evening after evening of expectation and excitement in your very own little "back yard" water. On the smart beat, rented for a formidable sum, you feel that you must work hard all the time when there is the chance of a fish. After all you are paying a lot for your two weeks and, though you are not fishing for money so that your catch can cover your rent, you can help to reduce expenses by selling some of your fish. Then there is the far greater urge to fish hard from the knowledge that your time is so limited that every day must play its part. Owning your own little bit you have none of this. There is no high rent to pay. Fish revenue does not enter the picture for every fish in prospect is already bespoken for the household larder or as present to relative or friend. As to the number of fish you expect, unlike the smart beat where the record is all-important, you don't care a damn for this is entirely your own domestic affair. You fish when you want; how you want; making your own rules, if any, as to fly, bait, prawn or worm according to weather and water conditions. The tenant who rents is bound by the proprietor's rules which may well restrict to fly only or no spinning after the end of March, or never prawn or worm. Yet in April the unfortunate tenant may be faced with a river in flood and with water so coloured as to make fly quite hopeless. A well fished worm in the high brown water or a big spinning bait could provide the only hope but, alas, the rules forbid and there is nothing to be done except go back and sit in front of the fire in the hotel lounge. Take the case of a late June or July rent. The water is dead low and the temperature nearly 70°. The fish can be seen lying in the pools and you have tried every fly in your box and they just won't look at it. The prawn is the only hope but on this particular river it is absolutely forbidden. Again, the hotel lounge or bar is the sole answer. Of course this prohibition does not extend to all rivers and if you are lucky enough to have a Tweed rental you can mount your prawn for on the Tweed it is a recognised bait.

The first fishing we owned was in 1950 when we bought Hendersyde, the house and park of about 100 acres but not the famous Hendersyde fishings. These were far beyond our means but the real estate company which had bought the estate from the Executors of the late Lady Peel wanted very much to sell off the house and park, leaving them with the main fishings and some farms. To induce us to buy house and park the company agreed to the sale of half a mile of the left bank which ran below the park wall bordering the Kelso-Coldstream main road. What they sold us was considered, in relation to the famous lower Hendersyde water, an almost no-good stretch. Together with the opposite bank that belonged to the Duke of Roxburghe there were really only three pools with a doubtful fourth. On our side we had the island which, for reasons I will explain, would not hold fish. The Winter Cast on the Duke's side was the best of the whole stretch. Below this was the Mill Stream fished from a boat and from either side. At the bottom of the stretch was the not-much-good Ferry Pool. "Bobo" Roxburghe, as he was known to all friends, rented us the opposite bank, so we had a small complete fishing unit, poorly thought of as it was. The lower Hendersyde water gave an average of over three hundred fish a year. Our water was hardly ever fished because it was not thought worth while compared with the main fishings downstream. I set about doing what I could with what is now known as the Upper Hendersyde beat. The banks were cleared. I sank some concrete blocks to break up the water where I found a stream was too smooth. Above all, I made sure the water was thoroughly fished. The results were well worth while. When conditions were good in February, March and April I could count on a spring fish from either the Winter Cast or the Mill Stream. One bitter March day when the snow was driving horizontally onto the water and the ice-coated line freezing in the rings of the rod Tony Milward and I had nine fish out of the Winter Cast before lunch. We chucked it then because we were both too cold to go on. Tony said that he had to soak in a boiling bath for an hour to restore some feeling to his frozen limbs. There was one unpleasant feature of our water which was the reason why fish would not lie in the Island pool at the top of the beat. Pollution from Kelso town. At that time in the fifties Kelso had no proper sewage treatment plant. If you fished between 8 a.m. and noon your fly or bait was more than likely to get caught up in used lavatory paper as it floated down accompanied by raw sewage. I am happy to record that Kelso now has a proper disposal plant and once again fish lie in the island pool in good clean and pure water. Our best year's total during the seven years at Hendersyde was a hundred and we averaged around sixty. Today Upper Hendersyde takes its place as one recognised spring beats; except, sad to say, now there are mighty few spring fish anywhere on the Tweed. The river seems to be reverting to what it was at the beginning of the century: a fine autumn river with a run of heavy fish in October and November. In 1958 business affairs made it necessary for me to be constantly back and forth to London so we decided to sell. Sir John Gilmour, a friend and neighbour, bought the fishing for his son "Sandy" Gilmour who still owns it. "Bobo" kindly allowed me to transfer the lease of his bank and Sandy has done improvements that I would like to have done but could not afford. He has built out a concrete spit at the head of the Mill Stream which has concentrated the water flow and wonderfully improved the catch. Then on the left bank he has built a charming fisherman's bungalow with rod room and a sitting room for owners' use.

In the Hendersyde years I learnt quite a lot about the Tweed up as far as Bemersyde and at some time or other have fished most of the beats either as guest or tenant. Best day ever for me on the Tweed or any other river was on the Mertoun Water just below the house. Lord Ellesmere, as he then was and is now Duke of Sutherland, had kindly asked me to stay and to fish the next day. Wading the House Pool was safe and easy. I started at the head of the pool at about 10 a.m. using a Canadian No. 7 Moose Hair Fly. It was a lovely May morning and the river was full of fish. My hostess told me at lunch that she had come out several times onto the grass lawn which looks down on the river just to see if her guest was all right. Each time she looked she saw my rod bent double into a fish, and so it went on all the morning. The score was eleven. In the afternoon the fish closed right down so far as taking the fly. From the boat worked by the fisherman I managed another three on a prawn. I recount this fourteen in the day in no boastful spirit, but only to offset a long record of blank days on nearly every beat I have ever fished. I did have something of a "runner-up" on Lower Floors when "Bobo" Roxburghe kindly asked me for an afternoon. I had been ill and was not allowed to wade but fished from the boat. The fish were in a good mood and we had nine by 6 p.m.

Upper Hendersyde was finished by end of May so for several Julys I took Rutherford which lies just below Mertoun. Here, when the fly was no good the prawn saved the situation. If the fish were on the prawn it was a lot of fun with light tackle and perhaps one shot for weight. Cast upstream, let it sink then slowly draw in the line. Sometimes a fish would rush madly at the prawn; sometimes they would knock it, nibble at it and play about for long nerve racking minutes. You could feel all this on your line and tactics were to remain absolutely still, just giving a little line when the fish asked for it. Finally the fish swims steadily off. You feel the line being pulled out and then you have to make up your mind to have the courage to strike. It is a bit of a gamble. He may spit it out or it maybe that he has taken it so that when you strike your prawn hooks go home in his jaw. One thing I did learn at Rutherford. If the fish don't want a prawn don't go on but just pack it in for that day so far as prawning is concerned.

Next venture in salmon fishing ownership came about in a lucky way. I had asked several relations and friends if ever they heard of some fishing, going for a reasonable price, please to let me know. Though we were back living in London always I longed for some base in Scotland. Through devious ways I learnt in 1960 that a beat on the Deveron called Ardmiddle might be for sale. There was once an Ardmiddle House, a Scotch walled garden, an estate and about a mile of fishing on the right bank, some two miles above Turiff. Now the estate had gone, the house demolished and only the garden and the fishing left. This latter had been bought for how much I do not know by Captain Hay of Delgaty Castle near Turiff. Captain Hay was not a fisherman but even when he bought it the Ardmiddle Water had been neglected for years. The banks were overgrown and weeds, reeds and rushes allowed to flourish. There were no paths along the banks which needed a lot of attention. I believe Captain Hay had some local arrangement that allowed a few interested people to fish for £1 per day: indeed I heard tell of someone reported to have caught thirty fish in the season. But, by and large, you could say Ardmiddle was in pretty poor shape with an owner ten miles away who was no fisherman. I got in touch with Captain Hay and we arranged to meet on the river bank one particular afternoon. Here came my great luck. The family friend who first told me about Ardmiddle lived nearby. She had kindly asked me to lunch and thought I should meet Mr Henderson who knew and had actually fished the beat. This was my first meeting with one who has become, with his delightful wife, a real friend of my family and myself. Bill Henderson is of a farming family and himself farmed in a big way at Seggat, a few miles off. Since then they have handed Seggat to their eldest son and now live on Speyside. As well as a highly efficient and successful farmer Bill was a mad keen fisherman and first class shot. At lunch he fired me with the Ardmiddle possibilities if taken seriously in hand. After lunch the whole party of us went over to Ardmiddle to meet Captain Hay. Here was a man 6' 6" tall and broad in proportion who always wore the kilt, bare headed and without socks or shoes. The latter he never wore, walking all over his fields and farm barefooted. Sandy hair and moustache, hirsute from top to toe, clear blue eyes, his character was as firm and grand as his appearance. The life work of he and his late wife has been the restoration of Delgaty Castle. With his own hands, and very little outside help, he has secured the castle fabric, done the decorative masonry work and interior reconstruction. It is a terrific achievement for one man and Delgaty Castle is now marked on every map of Scotland and guide book as an historic Scottish castle not to be missed. Captain Hay walked us over the stretch. He was frankness itself about his lack of real interest in Ardmiddle as a fishery. I think he had bought it a few years before because it went cheaply and no one seemed to want it. The fishing record had been badly kept but taking everything into consideration Bill and I thought that, cleaned up and fished regularly, one might get 60 or thereabouts in the season. After some very genteel bargaining we agreed on a price of £8,000. At this time I did not have £8,000 for a fishing but my good friend Tony Somers helped out with the purchase and became joint owner. Later he generously allowed me to repay his help so I became sole owner. One of Captain Hay's activities was a small building company so I asked him to undertake the contract for what I wanted; more than just a fishing hut but a small pavilion. I chose a site overlooking a pool and where we found remains of what in years gone by must have been a fishing shelter hut. My pavilion had to have a covered over balcony, one decent sized sitting room, a separate Elsan, a cooking stove, a washing sink, cupboards, and rod rack. All this Captain Hay did splendidly for about £375. Our furniture and crockery, cooking utensils cost another £35 or so, thanks of course to Woolworths. Anyhow there we were in business for a total, including legal costs, of £8,595. My good luck continued. I asked two things of Bill Henderson. Would he organise some of his farm labour to clear up the banks and build paths and little bridges where needed from top to bottom of the beat, and would he use his farm machinery to cut a road down to the fishing pavilion, for at the moment there was only an overgrown path. All this Bill did for me, just charging base labour costs. Next we planned the fishing of the beat. I knew any increase in capital value would depend on a three or five year average. I did not want to let. I only wanted the pools fished regularly and well. Would Bill take on organising a team of rods to fish daily. For Bill and his family, the river was, of course, theirs. We agreed the visiting rods should pay nothing and one fish in three would be theirs. The other two were to be sold for my account. Having arranged all this so happily I turned to the question of where I could stay when I came up. Once more I was lucky. Robin Duff, laird of Old Meldrum House, in Old Meldrum, was running his big house as a hotel. Being a "bon viveur" the cellar was fine and Robin, himself a cook of cordon bleu quality, gave us wonderful meals.

How Robin found — and still finds — time to run Old Meldrum House, be on Local Authority Boards, be an ex-County Councillor, a B.B.C. voice on Brains Trust and like programmes, take a leading part in the musical life of Aberdeenshire, I just do not know. For myself and family as well as my fishing guests Old Meldrum House was a centre of friendship and comfort. One of my chief regrets when I sold Ardmiddle is that I can no longer find reasons to go and stay with Robin.

The fishing came up to and exceeded my hopes and expectations. I managed to get up to Ardmiddle quite fairly often and fishing alongside Bill we had lots of fun and excitement. There was our best pool, lovely to fish — called Peninsular — which served me well nearly every time I went down it. I allowed any legitimate bait but, by custom, we always went over the water with fly first before going to minnow or prawn. In really dirty water the worm came into its own. So for nearly eight years Ardmiddle gave me great friendship — with Bill Henderson and his family — and good fishing from February through to the end of October, though in the last month all red hens were returned to the water. During my last three years of ownership Devron riparian owners lived under a threat that if implemented would have spoilt the river fishing. The Aberdeen authorities cast envious eyes on the Deveron Water. They coveted it for new housing estates. They admitted the water flow and river depth would be lowered. Even so, they said, valuable fishings must give way to social needs. "Yes," we owners replied, "but why build a huge reservoir at the head of the river and then dam up our water." "Why not pump it out right down towards the river mouth?" "Oh no," said authority. "Our experts say that for lots of reasons that would not do. Expense of pumping would be more than extracting from a loch-reservoir." "What about the millions to be spent on building the loch-reservoir?" we asked.

"Well Hooked": Serpentine River

Upper Camp, Restigouche

The Restigouche

Our Seaplane at Anchor

The Maestro Gives Directions

Hunt River, Labrador

Trying for the Big One — Restigouche

A Big One Caught

"Safely in the Net": Gander

The author

Off To Work — Gander

"Interest on capital." "How does that compare with pumping costs?" — no answers.

A private Bill was promoted by the Aberdeen authorities. Our protests were overidden. Our alternative spurned. The Secretary of State ordered an Enquiry. The Inspector reported not in favour of Aberdeen. The Secretary of State overruled his Inspector. The Secretary of State's Department partnered the Aberdeen authority. The Parliamentary Select Committee considering the Bill sent up three members under chairmanship of the late Lord Mansfield who themselves conducted an inquiry. They found in favour of pumping and against the Loch proposal. Now it became a political issue. Would the Secretary of State defy the findings of a Parliamentary Committee. The Secretary of State capitulated. Aberdeen was defeated. There would be no great loch-reservoir. The Deveron was saved as a lovely river giving sport and pleasure to citizens of every section of the community — and water is quite happily extracted by pumping from a station just above Turrif without any serious effects on the fishing.

So much for the "experts". In a life that has had much to do with "experts" in the world of flying I have long learnt never to accept an expert's opinion without making the experts justify their views and proposals to a dumb inexpert like myself.

In the course of evidence at the Enquiry an official of the Scottish Office was asked what capital value he put on Deveron salmon. His reply was "£200 a fish". I put this cutting away most carefully for future use. After we bought our Sutherland home of Tressady I found Ardmiddle too far to go to. Now we had fishing all around us, the Brora, Shin and our own little spate river, the Fleet. Meanwhile for £4,000 I had bought the bank opposite Ardmiddle from the executors of the late Sir George Abercrombie so now I could offer any purchaser both banks and an average for three years of a hundred fish (including of course the red autumn hens returned to the water). I sold for, I think, £20,000 in 1966 fishings that stood me in around £13,000 for both banks. When the question of C.G.T. came up I was able to say that in 1964 my fishing had yielded 100 fish which by the Government official's own enquiry evidence gave me a capital value of £20,000 prior to the introduction of this tax. Therefore no C.G.T. was payable. Thus the policy of no renting but constant daily fishing paid off.

One final word on the finance of salmon fishing ownership. "Bobo" Roxburghe told me that after paying rates, taxes, maintenance, and ghillies' wages for his absolutely first class Tweed water which he could always let at that time at a high figure, with prospective tenants queuing up to be on the list, he doubted if he made 1% on the value of the fishing.

There is no great fortune in ownerships. You may break even and get your own fishing for nothing, but little more. Even so, I believe ownership gives an indefinable pleasure of possession and thus I have now answered in some detail the question I asked at the beginning of this chapter.

CHAPTER THIRTEEN

"When Shall I Dwell With Worms"

Shakespeare, Henry VIII

THIS is the tale of a visit to Iceland but also concerns worms. Now I like a bit of worming as much as the next man: but worming must be kept in its right fishing compartment and not allowed free play when other more subtle and skilful ways of catching salmon are expected to be practiced. Give me a river in flood with dirty brown water coming down bank high. Such fish as are in the river are working their way upstream. In all probability one or two may show head and tail in mid stream, a sure sign that feeling the new rising water they are "running". It's no good thinking you will catch one as it moves up river with whatever lure or bait you care to try. The real hope is to find a resting fish in some backwater or protected corner clear of the strong current. Take out from the depth of your pocket that old tobacco tin and pull out one or even two luscious great worms which you, or some younger member of your family, have found by turning over that manure heap in the farmyard. Thread two on a hook, put a lump of lead on the leader and cast upstream in the limited area free of the main stream. Keep your finger on the line ready to feel that first little twitch coming up from somewhere far below. It is either a salmon, a sea trout or brown trout. You don't care about the "brownies" but do care about the other two. The twitches develop into definite tugs on the line and go on getting stronger. As each tug gets stronger so the fish deep in the muddy waters is getting keener and keener until at last it makes up its mind to "have a go". Now firmly and positively you feel it swimming away. The line moves across the water's surface. Give it a couple of yards of line then strike and strike hard. By now the fish will have swallowed the worm and the chances are that the hook is firmly embedded well down the gullet. After that it is all easy going and in due course you net the salmon. Surely you have been fully justified in using the worm as bait for in no other way would you have had the slightest hope of success that day.

It is on a well-known river in Iceland that I have seen the worm used not in the flood conditions I have just described but alongside and in rivalry to the small fly and floating line usual technique. For two successive Julys Tony Somers and I rented two rods on the Laxa Ein recognised as about the best salmon river within easy motor drive from Reykjavik. We flew from London by Iceland Airways Jet and at the airport Customs met our first difficulty of that first year. We knew better for the second year. "Where," asked the Customs official, "are your certificates of disinfection for your lines, casts and waders?" We had none for no one had warned us about this. But the Icelandic authorities were right and wise to insist on all steps that would prevent the introduction to their waters of the U.D.N. salmon disease, still, alas, all too prevalent in many of our rivers. Fortunately we were being met by the chief of the fishing syndicate-club where we were going. On his promising on word of honour that our boots and tackle would be fully disinfected before we started to fish the next day, our gear was released. Picking up two self-drive Volkswagens, with some navigation difficulty and several road errors, we were finally on the main highway from Reykjavik to Borgenes. It took us about an hour to reach the road bridge over the Laxa Ein. Away on the other side of the river standing some fifty yards back from the water we saw the white buildings; headquarters of the fishing. Our chief was a delightful and enterprising man who knew London well and spoke perfect English. The ten miles or so of fishing belonged to a whole lot of small farmers, each owning fishing rights on his little bit of land. Our chief had cleverly and with much difficulty managed to rent all the water from the multitude of owner-farmers. He then divided the fishing into the Upper and Lower. In turn he divided each of these into four beats and put two rods on each beat. Thus every day there could be sixteen rods fishing. If the weather had behaved rightly there could have been plenty of fishing for all but, alas, on both summers we were there not enough rain had fallen to allow any but the odd salmon to reach the Upper half. Finally we finished up some twelve rods on the Lower half. Three to a beat was too many except for one saving factor. Of our twelve only two others and myself fished with fly. The others all fished the whole day with worm. Each rod would go to his allotted beat, pick his worming spot and stay put there all day. This meant for any fly fisherman virtually the free run of the beat, always avoiding the small area around each worm exponent.

Our quarters were in a school and extremely comfortable. Very sensibly with schools closed all the summer, the Icelandic Government uses school buildings as hotel-hostels. Each of us had a single room with running hot and cold. There were enough bathrooms and a splendid sauna. The washrooms, lavatories and bathroom were painted white and kept meticulously clean. All fishing guests sat for meals at two long tables. Food was excellent and Icelandic beer included "on the house". Breakfast 7.30 a.m. onwards: in at noon for midday meal: out again at 4 p.m. and fish till 9 p.m. when everyone was supposed to come off the river. The day's catch with your name on it was put in an electrically operated deep freeze. In the living room there was a blackboard on which each evening you read what was to be your next day's beat. To be posted to the Upper Water with no fish was a waste of half a day. Tony Somers and I invented a phrase for a posting to the Upper Water which very quickly became common usage among the fisher-guests. It was known as "being sent to Outer Mongolia". We only had six days before us so by the time we had wasted three half days Tony and I went on strike. We had not come all the way and paid a good many U.S. dollars to fish half-time. We were not alone in our protests about "Outer Mongolia" for others joined us. The chief saw our point, though the poor fellow could not be blamed for the water level.

He finally agreed to put another rod, making three on each of the Lower beats. However, one more worm angler meant just one more fixed position so to a fly fisherman this extra rod made little difference.

Our fellow guests were a cosmopolitan lot. Mostly Americans: two complete families, and several N.A.T.O. U.S. Army and Air Officers stationed at Klepavik, two Italians and some Icelanders. We all seemed to get on together but the worm anglers were liable to suffer from periodic acute shortages of worms. In the treeless volcanic soil there were no worms to be dug for. Somewhere in Reykjavik an enterprising fellow had started a worm farm. The demand from all over Iceland was terrific. He must have been making a fortune in this country where so many fished with worm only. From our headquarters an emissary was sent daily to the worm farm to buy supplies for sharing out among the dedicated wormers. So expensive and precious were these that when anyone left he was expected to bequeath any unused to his fellow fishermen.

Worm fishing was usually done on a salmon fly rod. The cast needed was often only a short one for the pools lay literally at the feet of the fishermen. The number of salmon caught was high. My friend Tony Somers, who had done but little fly fishing, very rightly from his point of view, soon saw that if he was to enjoy the thrill of a salmon on the end of his line in that rocky fast moving river he would do better to abandon fly and take to the worm.

In our six days he landed twenty-seven fish averaging about 7 lbs. For myself, sticking to the fly, I had twenty two of about the same average weight. I record one interesting economic fact. Our hire car cost about £30. Our catch was taken to the market and I had enough cash from the sale of fish to pay one night's expenses in the best hotel in Reykjavik and to pay off the hire car costs.

Of course, there are finer rivers, richer in fish than our Laxa Ein but we only had one week to spare (anyhow we could not have afforded the U.S. dollars for another); we knew no one and here was the easiest most accessible river for two strangers to fish.

For me it was a week of glorious isolation with fly in the midst of a world of wriggling worms.

CHAPTER FOURTEEN

Coincidence—Or What?

THE Lower Brora yields fish. Always it yields never failing interest to fishermen. Sometimes this interest is crowned with success. More often it is a case of gloom and despair. The river runs from Loch Brora in a straight three miles to the North Sea and very little more allowing for its meanderings through rich farmland. It has 26 pools and given the right level of water has plenty of good holding places. Personally I have found it the most disappointing river I know. Each March or early April I take two rods on the south bank for a fortnight. There seems to be a hoodoo over my two weeks. Either the river is too low and there are no fish up, or it is in flood and every fish is running hard up river, through Loch Brora into the Upper Brora and the River Blackwater, far the most going to the latter. Still down on my stretch there is always a chance that a thirty pounder will seize my fly. If in my two weeks two rods get six salmon I feel I am doing very well.

It was a bitter March day a few years ago that what I now relate took place. All day I had flogged the pools without a touch. Not a fish had shown yet I knew there must be fish in the river for there had been a good rise from two days' rain to bring fresh fish in from the sea. By now it was nearly 4 p.m. I was tired and frustrated. Once more down the Ford pool and I would call it a day. As I started down the pool I said to myself out loud: "Oh, please God let me have just one chance". Then I thought to myself: was I a wicked man to appeal to God for my own selfish pleasure and in hopes that I could kill off one of God's living creatures—a lovely salmon which in its way must have for itself a life of value. As I worked down the pool I started within myself something of a philosophic argument. Was my little prayer for a fish an abuse of the use of prayer? Was catching and killing fish an abuse of nature? I decided to tackle this second question first. I recalled that this was no new moral problem for one who loves fishing and shooting. It had often given me worry until some months before when I had been thinking along these lines I had brought to mind that a friend had told me there were references in the Bible which said in effect, that to catch fish and kill birds was quite in accord with Christian teaching provided they were for feeding mankind. I knew I should feel much happier within myself if when enjoying catching a fish or shooting a pheasant I could justify to myself this issue of morality in my use of rod or gun. There and then I had decided I must seek out the exact biblical quotation. In the House of Lords I tackled my good friend the Rev. Lord Soper, a man to the Left of the Left, but a character respected and loved by members of all parties. We have over twenty Bishops of the Church of England who sit as Lords Spiritual but they scare me stiff and I would never dare to put to one of them a personal question on a theological matter. To me they always seem a select and segregated section of the House. The only time I ever feel something in common with these Lords Spiritual is when in the Peers' bar I find one or two taking the sort of spirit I enjoy before lunch, but I felt the Peers' bar is no place for religious discussion. So it was to Lord Soper, the least frightening and most human of men I took my difficulty. Without a moment's hesitation he replied: "Oh, you must mean Luke V verses 5 and 6". I went straight off to the Library to look up the passage when Simon said to Jesus: "Master we have toiled all day and have taken nothing. Nevertheless at thy word I will let down the net." Simon and the fishermen obeyed Jesus' instructions to have another go. They got so many fish the net broke. I did not aspire so high. Just one fish would safely see me through my need. Then to justify my shooting I turned to Deuteronomy, chapter 14, verse 11 where we are bidden to eat the flesh of clean birds, such as fowl, pheasant, duck or partridge. So as with fishing I felt I had biblical clearance and could now go ahead with shot gun for that current and subsequent seasons.

By now I was half way down the pool and not a sign of a fish, so I turned my mind to my first question. Was I selfish and was it an abuse of prayer that I had asked God to grant me a fish. And anyhow was such an appeal likely to have any result? Even if it was a selfish request I felt sure it would be accepted under the circumstances as a reasonable plea from a humble petitioner. Like so many of us who pray, when our prayer is met we forget to say "Thank you". So there and then I pledged

90

myself to render thanks if on this occasion my prayer was granted. On the issue of whether my request would be granted I had to try to keep an open mind. I could only tell myself that I am a very humble believer in the power of prayer. For many years I have found strength and comfort in Tennyson's lines in "Morte d'Arthur". "Pray for my soul. More things are wrought by prayer than this world dreams of."

Now I was three-quarters down the pool and still blank when I brought to mind the answer one of our very recent Archbishops gave when asked what he thought about the power of prayer. His reply was wonderfully simple and direct: "When I pray coincidence happens. When I don't it doesn't."

I had reached the end of the pool. There were only a few more yards to cover. I cast a long line into the tail. A fierce tug as a beautiful twelve pound salmon fresh up from the sea seized my fly and after a fine fight, was duly netted.

Coincidence. Was it?

CHAPTER FIFTEEN

It's True—I Swear It Is

THE salmon rich waters of Dornoch Firth flow into the Kyle, or estuary, at Sutherland's Bonar Bridge. The Kyle serves no less than four first class rivers, Shin, Oykel, Cassley and Carron. It was one summer on the Carron that I had the extraordinary experience I wish to record. The Carron is a medium-sized spate river running up from the Kyle into the hills of Central Highlands with about eighteen miles of fishable water. It was on the up-river stretch of my good friend Admiral Sir Geoffrey Robson that the event occurred. Thanks to the ever generous Sir Geoffrey I was one of four rods on his Amat Water and our catch for that day amounted to ten fish. It was a hot August day following two days of rain which had made a big river calling for a sinking line and 1½" lure, and during the morning I had been lucky in landing two fish. Then back to a lovely lunch in the lodge preceded by true Naval hospitality.

"Another Pink Gin?" "Yes." I did. Then some fine red wine followed afterwards by a glass of port. By now I was more than ready to relax in place of starting an afternoon's fishing. However, the keeper and I got into the Land Rover and went down to the Barn pool, a pool of great character with a fast rocky run-in fanning out into a smooth glide the width of the river with a run-off at the tail which is all a fisherman could ever ask for.

The afternoon was hot. The sun shone from a clear sky. There were hours of lovely fishing ahead but I decided, on balance, to ask the keeper to go down the pool first while I relaxed on the grass bank for half an hour's easy. I lay down, closed my eyes and must have dozed for when I looked up there beside me I saw a closely written sheet of paper which I certainly had not noticed before. I picked it up and saw at once it was a letter. I was curious and intrigued as to how a letter could suddenly appear beside me, so I decided to read it. I still remember all it said.

> "From: Miss Spawnetta Silverscale
> The Barn Pool
> River Carron
> AMAT.

The Editor
Salmon and Smolt
The Kyle
Bonar Bridge

Dear Mr Editor,

I am a young grilse who has been swimming, off and on, for three years in our Kyle. Knowing your paper is read by salmon of no less than four rivers, I feel that the story of my frightening Carron experience may act as a warning to my fellow salmon.

In company with a great number of sisters, brothers, cousins and friends I came into the Kyle from the sea this July intending to re-visit my birth place at the head of the Carron. I must be frank with you and admit that 'Sex had reared its ugly head' for I felt very sexy and longed to start a family of my own. Now my mother had explained to me the facts of fish life when she warned me with the words: 'Spawnetta dear,' she said, 'when you go on your travels upstream take care. If you ever find yourself alone up a burn look very carefully at any of the boys who swim towards you. Beware of those "queers" who tell you they are just old kipper baggots—not faggots—but really just the same for with them you will never have any lovely parr. They are no good to you so look for a fine young male as your mate.'

Now Mr Editor I must tell my story about my Carron tragedy. Mother decided this year to swim upstream once again with the rest of us for she is a remarkable salmon. Twice widowed and still she wants to return to the river. After her first marriage and the birth of her children she dropped back to the sea. She tells me she was starved; her looks gone, her figure lost. Fresh fish she passed on their way upstream jeered at this ghost of a once lovely fish and shouted: 'Poor old Keltie', a most insulting expression in our fish world. All around her exhausted kelts were dying but mother refused to give in. So now on our travel upstream she is alongside of me ready to produce another family.

I confess that when two years ago as a smolt, I met my stepfather I did not take to him. He had a horrid hooked lower jaw and his skin was a dark red. To little me he seemed a great giant who spent half his time chasing away any young male who dared to swim towards our private patch of gravel. You will understand why I hated this great bully-boy of 14 lb when I tell you he suddenly made a pass at me who was far too young to think about laying eggs. Mother was furious and they had a good fight which scared away every other fish from their marriage bed.

To go on with my story. We started up-river with sisters, cousins and some of the boys as well. Alas, we could not get far as the water got shallower and shallower and very warm. All we could do was to laze at the bottom of a pool waving our tails and fins just waiting.

Then the rain came bringing lovely fresh water and like a pack of school girls we rushed upstream. As we went we jumped for joy and played like porpoises.

It took quite a time to get up here to the Barn where the horrid event took place. Mother had warned me to swim clear of and never be tempted by lovely bits of colour flashing past my nose which I might think were little fish and snap at. 'Don't be lured by yellow, red or blue,' she said.

It was just as well I remembered her words when a beautiful bright piece of colour crossed just in front of me. I was about to go for it when her warning checked me just in time. I turned away but too late to warn my brother who was swimming alongside of me. He bit at it and the next moment I saw he was in terrible danger. He rushed up and down the pool. He jumped clear of the water. I could do nothing. I called for mother but she must have been somewhere else in the pool for she never came. After some minutes my brother was so exhausted he just turned on his back. Then a strange contraption came out from the bank and scooped him up and out of sight. We never saw him again.

In these moments of anguish I remembered another warning mother had given us. It consisted of a vulgar ditty that she had picked up in the sea from some rather common mackerel—

Girls Girls, Girls. Take a tip from me
Never trust a sailor an inch above the knee.

At once I felt I must shout out another warning so loud that the vibrations of my tail carried right across the pool—

Girls, Girls, Girls. Take a tip from me
Never trust a lure whatever it seems to be.

With love from your sad little
SPAWNETTA."

I heard a shout and in an instant was wide awake. It was the keeper who was into a fish. But the letter beside me had vanished.

CHAPTER SIXTEEN

The Silly Little River

FOR ten years I have had a passionate love affair with a river. It is in Sutherland; it is only fifteen miles long; runs from the hills around Lairg and empties into the North Sea at Mound; more often than not is almost dry; yields only about a hundred fish a season and was described by a friend as "a silly little river". But, even so, I love this river Fleet. I have been lucky enough to fish fine beats on the Spey, Dee and Tweed, yet on the all-too-rare times when the Fleet is in order I would choose it before the great ones. It can certainly be labelled a non-U river. It can be fickle, unreliable, seductive and fascinating. Our Tressady Lodge has two miles of the north bank running from Rogart village railway station, where you still ask for the train to be stopped, upstream to where fishing ends and the stream turns itself into a small burn. The strongest link in the chain of my affection is what I tried to set out in the chapter "Would you like to own a fishing". In this I wrote that I would rather own my own little backyard of fishing than be a short term tenant on one of the great and famous rivers. I should certainly get more fish on well known rivers but I should not have the pride of possession of my own water, free to fish just when and how I want. I have learned the Fleet's peculiarities. I have got to know every salmon lie at different water levels. I have only to look at one particular rock opposite Tressady drive gates to know whether she has risen or fallen. Too often we wait through weeks of summer drought for the rains that never seem to come to what is about the dryest spot in Scotland. I don't believe there can be anywhere else where the B.B.C. news weather forecast chart is studied more closely than at Tressady Lodge. A "low" coming in from the west is for us like a doctor's bulletin "Prospects for recovery are good".

We don't expect fish in our water until the second spate in July or August but the trouble is that some years that second spate just never comes. Early spates; a good season—maybe twenty-five fish off our bank. No spate; no fish and a blank season.

Once in 1965 Tressady had its record of 54. Three times in ten years we were over twenty but in the fishing book there are recorded too many blank, or just-on blank seasons. The river is so narrow that you can cast across it with a short line but we have a sensible arrangement with the other bank that divides the stretch into two with a change over at lunch time so both parties have the chance of fishing all the water every day. We need twenty-four hours rain to give two days fishing. One night's rain and maybe half a day before she becomes unfishable once more until more rain and yet another rise of water. You should be on the water literally on the hour she starts to come up. In Tressady Lodge a morning after a night's good rain is a time of real excitement. A quick breakfast and I am in the gunroom with George Murray, our keeper, who gives his river report. Simplicity is the keyword of Tressady fishing— no heavy fishing bags of tackle to sling over shoulder, no waders. Put on gum boots; seize a net, a box of flies, spool of nylon, a light nine foot six inches sea trout rod and we are off in a minute aboard the Land Rover. We go straight to the Stepping Stones pool, called this because before there was an iron suspension bridge the only way crofters and shepherds could cross dry was to jump from one stone to another. When the water laps the top of the stones you can bet on getting fish. I start at the head working down the sixty yards of the pool foot by foot. I know exactly which cast is almost sure to rise a fish. Three steps down from the head and I rise a salmon. It won't come again. It is one of those "once-ers". Two more steps and I am into a good fish. When it jumps I see it is quite fresh. Taken out of the net it registers 8 lbs. Towards the end of the pool we land another; this time a fairly coloured hen which is carefully unhooked and put back in the water. We take the Land Rover down a short distance to Upper Rovie. This is a long canal-like stretch of water of two hundred yards, deep with sluggish current but holding fish anywhere and must be searched from head to tail. We manage two more, one for me, one for George Murray. Three for the morning is good but by 5 p.m. the river has fallen and there is little use going on. Murray and I go back to the Lodge. Today the Fleet has showed herself worthy of all my affection.

George Murray is to me far more than keeper; far more than the first-class shot and fisherman that he is. He is my friend and companion who has shared with me splendid days on moor and river and taught me much, such as the little I know of the life and habits of grouse. He keeps the foxes down. Last year three vixens and cubs were eliminated as well as thirty-nine cats, some of the natural wild strain, and other domestic cats gone wild and all this to the great benefit of the young grouse. Murray is one of the Highland breed of men, sad to say, becoming ever fewer. Son of a Caithness keeper he has lived all his life in the Highlands except for war years overseas. Tall, broad, sandy hair he could never be taken for anything but what he is. One day as he and I argued over the world and its problems I said to him, "Tell me, why did you become a keeper? You could have made much more money in another job. Even now, if you cared to take on something else you could earn a lot more than I pay you." He was silent, thinking over his reply carefully with all the caution of a true Scot. "Well," he said, "for me it's a way of life." I understood how right he was in his answer. No other job, whatever the money rewards, would have given him the open life in glorious scenery close to the soil, with the birds and the animal life he loves around him. He has chosen to live for the indestructible things of true value, maybe not too rewarding materially but a life that allows a man to reach to true happiness. I know George Murray is so much more nature's gentleman than I could ever be.

I cannot finish with the Fleet without quoting August Grimble's classic book *Salmon Rivers of Scotland*. He writes that the Fleet has the unique feature that no other Scottish river can claim. It is the only river where salmon will take a fly in salt water. At its mouth there are heavy iron sluice gates. When the water flow from an up-river spate is sufficiently strong the gates open automatically from water pressure giving salmon waiting in the tidal salt water free passage. During the weeks we owners of the upstream beats long for more water. So also do the salmon waiting in the tidal estuary. With each high tide hopefully the shoals of salmon collect outside the gates. They jump and show and swim around before the poor things, thwarted once again, have to retreat back into the sea with the falling tide. Day after day they repeat their performance of hope until one happy day they find the sluice gates forced open and off up-river they rush. Below the sluice gates on the sea side is a concrete slipway and it is from here in the salt water that salmon can be caught on a fly. Some take normally but, fishing a large sunk fly, too many are foul hooked to the considerable disapproval of we Upper Fleet proprietors.

My hope is that I may have succeeded in somehow conveying why, in contrast to far finer and more rewarding fishings, the "silly little river Fleet" remains my love.

Somehow if, when I leave the "silly little river", I have the chance of fishing some famous river like the Dee or Spey I seem at once to become "incident prone".

I think back to a lovely summer holiday at Braemar Castle* which we had rented as sub-tenants from Lord Tweedsmuir. Here I was at Sluggan one afternoon around 5 p.m. all excited because a salmon had shown and it was the first seen in our Castle stretch for three weeks of low water and hot sun. I was determined to have a go at that fish with fly and then with prawn. I cast my fly but, alas, I hooked no salmon but an oyster-catcher in full flight. The bird must have been attracted by the mid-air glint of colour in the fly dressing. I had visions of having to play off the reel not a fish, but a bird in flight. It swooped down, then, when it must have felt the hook which caught in its leg, it rose and did an aerial half loop before collapsing on the shingle bank. When we managed to get the hook out of the bird's leg it flew away apparently none the worse. That was No. 1 incident of the day — and incidentally, we never caught that fish. The second incident that day, or night in this case, was far more serious and might easily have turned into a ghastly tragedy. At 3 a.m. in the morning my wife woke up to a strong smell of burning. By the time she had shaken me awake our room was filled with thick smoke coming up from between the floor boards, under the door and down the chimney. I got out to the landing and bellowed as loudly as I could, "Fire — Fire". My brother-in-law came from his room to join me on the landing. By this time I could see a thick cloud of smoke creeping up the spiral staircase to where we were standing. We had but one common thought. Get the children down the stairs from their rooms on the landing above. This stone stair was steep and narrow. It climbed from ground to the Castle turrets battlement roof. It was the only way down which the children and we could descend. These stairs ran up in a lefthand circle so that Hanoverian troops defending the

---

*Built in 1628, burnt down in the Jacobite rising of 1689, rebuilt in 1748 as a garrison post of the Hanoverian government to dominate the rebellious clans.

Castle could have their right sword arms free for action against the attacking enemy. We realised that if the thick smoke ever reached their landing the four children between four and nine, would be trapped, suffocated and burnt. Fortunately the governess in a room next to theirs had heard my alarm shout and acted without delaying a moment. By the time we were through the increasingly heavy stair-smoke with towels round our faces, she had the four in their nighties wrapped round with blankets and damp towels round mouths and noses. Before these still half asleep fairly scared kids knew what was happening we had them down those stairs, through the smoke and safely out on the lawn where they proceeded thoroughly to enjoy all the excitement and noise. We went back into the Castle and managed to get out some clothes and other personal possessions. The kitchen, pantry and other rooms were blazing well. The flames were taking hold of wooden floorboards, but could do nothing to solid stone walls except scorch the surfaces. With headlights blazing, siren hooting and bells ringing the Ballater Volunteer Fire Brigade roared up the drive. Unfortunately the fire engine stuck in the soft ground and the water pump pressure was only enough to send a stream one floor up. However, with what pressure there was and a lot of water carrying in buckets by a human chain the fire was got under control. With excited children loving it all, the night — or early dawn — finished with a fine party on the lawn with whiskey, beer and sandwiches for all concerned. Next morning came the inquest. How had the fire started and this did not take long to decide. We had a rather half-wit student to help with the holiday domestic chores. His last duty each night was to rake out the ashes of the cooking stove and empty them outside. This night he was lazy and careless. He raked out the almost red hot ashes into a bucket. Unfortunately he never noticed the bucket had a hole in it. Then instead of emptying the ashes outside he was lazy and shut the bucket in a housemaid's cupboard off the kitchen. Two rooms were burnt out and for weeks after everything we touched would be black and sooty. The second incident was over.

*   *   *

Over past years I have been allowed to pay court to what must be the richest three-quarters of a mile on the Aberdeenshire Dee in terms of fish caught. Every yard of Inchmalo, which lies on the north bank two miles above Banchory, can be fished and this in bedroom slippers. Opposite Inchmalo is the Lower Blackhall water and as you cast from your pleasant gravel path look across and see a very different picture. The figure opposite is in long waders with water up to his chest gingerly feeling his way through a chain of round and slippery rocks, each step made having first explored carefully with wading stick. At my age I am all for Inchmalo comfort.

Three hundred fish a year is pretty good going for just three-quarters of a mile and this Inchmalo does pretty regularly.

Until some two years ago Inchmalo belonged to a truly remarkable man, John Howlett, about whom Chapman Pincher has written in his foreword to this book. John Howlett's history of rise from a childhood of comparative poverty to riches is deserving of brief summary. From birth John had a bent for machinery blended with a sense of enjoyment of all that life offers allied to a moral integrity he never lost and inherited, I guess, from his Norfolk yeoman stock. At the age of fourteen he was an engineer apprentice at Sheffield on a salary of 4/- a week. By the outbreak of the First World War John had become first mechanic, then manager, then owner of a garage and small engineering repair shop at Lymington. The reputation of the engineering genius of this man filtered through to the Admiralty and War Office. John bid successfully for a contract to supply components for early aero engines. Then, seeing the piston and cylinder troubles of these engines he put his mind to the problems of remedy. With his own design for piston rings evolved by use of metals hitherto unthought of for the purposes he put them to, the Wellworthy piston ring came into existence and revolutionised design and usage of the internal combustion petrol engine. Fame and fortune came to John Howlett. By the end of the War in place of the old garage stood a fine modern factory. John became the biggest local employer of labour. He was made J.P. and served as Mayor of Lymington. Ups and downs of post-war booms and slumps passed him by. Motor car manufacturers had to have his Wellworthy products. So steadily his business prospered and expanded.

Again, probably from his early country upbringing John had an intense love for fishing and shooting. As his material resources expanded so could his sporting interests. It was soon after the end of the Second World War that the Inchmalo estate came on the market. It consisted of farms, timber, the fishing and a sombre great grey stone mansion. At the auction John bought the whole estate for around £140,000. Those were the days of real money. At once he sold off the farms, giving tenants first refusal. Next he found a buyer for the mansion which he had feared would be a white elephant. Standing timber was sold, other timber cut and when he had finished Inchmalo fishings stood him in around £10,000. Since John's death it has been sold for, I believe, around £230,000. At Inchmalo, in the pretty "Lairds Cast" cottage bungalow he built, John and his dear wife Gladys, sadly to follow John within a year, made any and every friend welcome to home and fishing. He could be called a bit of a rough diamond; not much education; not many social graces, but I do not think he or Gladys had an enemy in the world. He left us at ninety. As Chapman Pincher relates, having caught a salmon and shot a hare he came home, then sat down and died a happy and fulfilled man.

I found myself "incident prone" once again and this time on the Spey. Looking back on that day I really do not think it my fault that I offended and angered a well known Spey proprietor.

Soon after the War, with two friends I had rented Tulchan D beat, the bottom water of the lovely Tulchan stretch. We did well and on our last evening I was fishing the bottom of our beat, just upstream from a small ditch running into the river and which marked our boundary. On the other side of the ditch the Ballindaloch estate fishing started. The then Laird of Ballindaloch, dead now for many years, was a zealous guardian of his rights and made a habit of coming down in his car to watch the boundary to make sure not a Tulchan rod should go one step into his territory. As below the quite insignificant little boundary ditch a wire fence came down to the water and doubtless quite a few Tulchan fishermen must from time to time have mistakenly and not unreasonably, thought this fence was the boundary and hence the watching patrol of the laird. My fly landed just a couple of yards above the ditch and I was into a 20 lb salmon. I tried to work him upstream but this fish was no respecter of property rights for he insisted on swimming strongly downstream. I put on as much pressure as I dared, but even so down we went. I crossed the boundary ditch into the forbidden territory which, with a fish on, I was entitled to do. Out of the corner of my eye I saw a figure standing like a statue, leaning on his stick with a frozen look of disapproval on his face. I had to pass him and go further down. Finally I managed to gaff the fish and carried it up the path back to the Tulchan side. As I passed I lifted my cap — "A lovely fish, sir. Very lucky. Sorry I had to finish in your water." Not a smile, not a word of praise for 20 lb fish were not caught every day. The statue just looked at me with cold, very cold eyes. "Sorry yes — so am I. I had intended to fish that pool this evening. Now it is useless. Goodnight." The statue moved, got in his car and left without a look back. I felt squashed flat. I sought no more incidents like that one.

CHAPTER SEVENTEEN

Postscript to Gander — And To Hell With Age

THERE are not too many outdoor activities that allow over-seventies to declare with gusto *"To hell with age"*. Fishing is one of the few, for happy anglers, from Thames side float to Delfur on the Spey, can shout out this defiance. Maybe beyond seventy you must be willing to compromise, thinking twice before waist high wading in an early spring river. With eighty now beside me I look back to a March on the Lower Brora. It was the pig of a day and I was thankful my lower half was comfortably protected by the stream I was wading in while my top half faced a snow blizzard blowing horizontally straight into my face. February and March can best be given a miss except for casting from a boat. When the water warms and rivers are down to May and June levels, choose easy pools, never forget to use your wading stick, and once again you will feel like a two-year-old in terms of enjoyment. In the autumn go with your boatman who knows every lie and will position you so as to cover these without having to use full strength to cast a big lure on a long line off your 13′ 6″ double-handed rod.

All of us have heard: "For goodness sake be your age" but this need not mean you cannot still enjoy the loch or river at ninety — if you have not by then been carried off by some cause nothing to do with fishing.

In 1977, at seventy-nine, I don't think I ever enjoyed so much my visit to Newfoundland's Gander River which I have fished regularly since 1947. For ten days nephew Mark, who came out with me, and I lived in an angler's paradise. Out of bed at 5.30 a.m. each morning. Pull on pants and shirt, then full length thigh waders and at the head of the camp pool before 6 a.m. No need to wade deep in this 80 yards long swift-running stream or you would disturb the lies. Starting at the head we fished down literally foot by foot. Each morning before 7.30 one or both of us had a fish. We used light single-handed sea trout rods, floating line and something like a No. 7 or 8 size Blue Charm or Black Moose hair. We had neither gaff or net so each fish had to be played to a standstill then worked slowly from the deep to shallow water and finally beached. Back to the camp house and never did steaming hot coffee taste so good as the cup the camp cook had ready to greet us with. Wash, shave, dress and breakfast 8 a.m. By 8.30 one was sitting in the bow of an Indian canoe propelled by a 20 h.p. outboard engine and with a guide who knew every rock in the river and took you up rapids like a small aeroplane leaving the ground. The morning run was usually a mile or so up or downstream to one of the several holding pools. Back at noon for the all important "Guides' dinner hour". Out again around 2.30 p.m. In again at 5.30 for drinks and supper. The final outing was from 7.30 until dusk around 9.30 or 10 p.m. Bed by 10.30 and up again at 5.30 and so on for a glorious ten days. Nephew Mark when we left filled in the record cards asked for by the Government Fishery Department. One of the questions asked was: "For how many hours a day did you fish?" He entered for both of us "about nine". In my Gander chapter I described the amazing fighting qualities of these fish straight from the sea that take you down to the backing twice at least. They run small and that year I had an 8½ lb fish, the best of the season. On every one of our ten days one of us had fish and on several both of us had the legal limit of four fish a day for each rod. In the ten days between us we had 44 salmon. As fish caught by rod and line are not allowed to be sold, these were sent up river as welcome gifts to our host, and friends, guides' families, hospitals and old folk.

As years mount I find sense of pleasure becomes sharper. On the Gander one can rise the same salmon four or five times. Try fly after fly and finally either get him to take or put him down. Somehow this year it all felt more exciting than ever before. Each early morning I watched the sun rise slowly over the pine forest. One early morning a moose came down to water. A fish splashed in the pool. These, and much else became memories to be treasured. Maybe this accelerated sensitivity is because sub-consciously there is the knowledge this could be the last time and if proved not so there cannot be many summers beyond the present. It is that age carried with it the greater appreciation of what youth accepts with no thought beyond the present.

All we mortals have to accept those mental and physical changes that go with the onset of years. Provided one is spared the geriatric indignities that old age can bring to some, then activities can be adapted to such changes. I am fortunate that in my case, probably arising from early years of flying in open cockpit aircraft, my main age limitation is that of progressive deafness. Deafness can be a crashing bore for family and friends. One tends to shut oneself up in one's own little private world. The shock of realisation first hits you when you notice two of your family talking softly with the deliberate intention that you shall not hear what they are saying. Even so, I reckon I am lucky for I would prefer to be fairly deaf yet able to enjoy shooting and fishing rather than be confined to a wheel chair but able to hear the twittering of the sparrows. I find old age has some other pleasant compensations. Generally young folk are so kind and considerate to the elderly. The bother of travel: getting seats: looking after the luggage: these are taken off your shoulders. No need to tie your own flies on to the leader. No need to offer to take an oar rowing up the loch against a strong headwind. Just take a swig at your flask and say to yourself: "Let the others sweat it out".

If I may dare to leave a message to fellow fishermen entering what is termed "old age" it is that getting old need be no tragedy but can be an awful lot of fun.

Always remember "Life is for living".

Robert Browning wrote, "What's a man's age? He must hurry, that's all. Cram in a day what in his youth took a year to hold."